CW01431167

F1
GENERATIONS

F1

THE LEGACY AND FUTURE OF BRITISH DRIVERS

GENERATIONS

Frank Worrall

bl!nk

First published in the UK in 2025 by Blink Publishing
An imprint of Bonnier Books UK
5th Floor, HYLO, 105 Bunhill Row,
London, EC1Y 8LZ

Copyright © Frank Worrall, 2025

All rights reserved.

No part of this publication may be reproduced, stored or transmitted in
any form or by any means, electronic, mechanical, photocopying or otherwise,
without the prior written permission of the publisher.

The right of Frank Worrall to be identified as Author of this work
has been asserted by him in accordance with the Copyright, Designs and
Patents Act, 1988.

A CIP catalogue record for this book is available from the British Library.

Hardback ISBN: 9781788709873
Paperback ISBN: 9781788709880

Also available as an ebook and an audiobook

1 3 5 7 9 10 8 6 4 2

Design and Typeset by Envy Design Ltd
Printed and bound by CPI (UK) Ltd, Croydon CR0 4YY

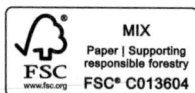

MIX
Paper | Supporting
responsible forestry
FSC
www.fsc.org FSC® C013604

Every reasonable effort has been made to trace copyright holders of
material reproduced in this book, but if any have been inadvertently
overlooked the publishers would be glad to hear from them.

The authorised representative in the EEA is
Bonnier Books UK (Ireland) Limited.
Registered office address: Block B, The Crescent Building
Northwood, Santry
Dublin 9, D09 C6X8, Ireland
compliance@bonnierbooks.ie

www.bonnierbooks.co.uk

*This book is dedicated to my wonderful brother, Stephen,
and my brilliant editor, Joe Hallsworth*

CONTENTS

CHAPTER 1

HINTERLANDS

Formula 1 may dazzle with its speed, glamour and seemingly endless abundance of cash, but the gladiators behind the wheel often have very different stories to tell of how they reached its pinnacle. The road to the grid is far from uniform. It is threaded together from sacrifice and struggle, sacrifice and privilege, from family determination and dynastic advantage, from the quiet devotion of parents who believed — and often from the accidents of birth that either opened doors or made those doors all but impossible to push through. The sport's paddock might look like one common stage of hedonistic excess, but its cast of characters are drawn from wildly different worlds. The lives of Lewis Hamilton, Lando Norris and George Russell show that contrast.

Lewis Hamilton's journey is a moving tale of an underdog becoming a world champion. Born in Stevenage in 1985, Lewis was raised predominantly by his mother, Carmen, a woman of remarkable resilience who had an iron will that seems to have been inherited by her son.

When Hamilton eventually broke into Formula 1, he was the first driver of Afro-Caribbean heritage to race in the sport. His childhood was comfortable but far from easy. The family lived on a council estate in Stevenage, 28 miles north of London. His father, Anthony Hamilton, fought to make ends meet, patching together income from IT contracting, dishwashing shifts and even hammering estate agent signs up outside houses. For years he worked three jobs at once. Every spare pound was poured into his son's karting career.

At the same time, racism was a constant presence for him and Lewis, at the racetrack, at the workplace and in the classroom.

Yet Anthony's devotion never wavered.

Lewis himself later looked back on those years with nostalgia: 'Back in my karting days, my dad and I were the only people who looked and sounded the way we did. None of the other kids seemed to come from a background like ours. Their parents all had money. From the age of nine or ten, I spent every weekend at a racetrack with Dad instead of hanging out with friends. He was my best friend.'

It was sacrifice and grit, rather than wealth or privilege, that propelled Hamilton upwards. That determination carried him from a modest flat in Hertfordshire to the top of the most lucrative sport in the world.

But the journey was not without controversy, nor was Hamilton's relationship with his home town straightforward.

In 2018, during a speech at the BBC Sports Personality of the Year Awards, he caused an uproar when he described Stevenage as 'the slums'. He quickly apologised, admitting he had chosen the wrong words, and insisted he felt proud of his roots, but the comment offended many in the town.

Stevenage Borough Council called his remark 'disappointing', pointing out that while the town had its struggles, it was far from a slum. It had been founded in 1946 as Britain's first 'new town', part of a post-war vision to rehouse bombed-out Londoners and create modern, planned communities. To Anthony Hamilton, who had worked and sacrificed there for decades, Stevenage was nothing to be ashamed of.

The wider Hamilton family story adds further background texture. Lewis's grandfather, Davidson, was a beloved figure back in Grenada, known for ferrying schoolchildren around the island in a battered Mitsubishi minibus with 'To God Be Glory' painted on its rear. Davidson's faith was woven through everything he did, and Lewis would later credit his own belief in divine guidance to those family roots. When Anthony bought his father a £20,000 replacement minibus years later, it was a tribute to both his hard work and his values.

Davidson had migrated to Britain in 1955 as part of a wave of Caribbean workers recruited by British Transport. He landed in a country where housing shortages meant landlords posted 'No Blacks' signs in windows. Like many, he moved where friends and compatriots already lived, at first staying with Trinidadians in west London.

In 1956, he married Agnes Mitchell in Fulham, and four years later their son Anthony was born. Davidson worked as a railway guard, a steady but unglamorous job. His second wife, Eulisia, was a devout Seventh-day Adventist whose principles of missionary work and Sabbath rest filtered into the family's outlook. Work ethic, faith and moral responsibility became part of their way of life.

Davidson always followed his grandson's career with pride, even confessing that a taste for racing might be in the blood. As a young man in Grenada, he tore around the island's winding roads on a motorbike before buying an Austin A40, only to be stopped for speeding at 40 in a 30 zone. 'That's when I learned to slow down,' he said later, laughing.

In July 2007, he travelled to Silverstone to watch Lewis race in a Formula 1 Grand Prix for the first time. Years earlier, he had only seen him in karts. Lewis was delighted: 'Grandad came to a karting event years ago, but never a Grand Prix. It's brilliant that he's here for this one.'

Anthony Hamilton's own childhood had been difficult. His mother died young and he grew up in west London facing racism and hardship. Those experiences gave him a toughness that he passed on to his son. Determined that Lewis would not be bullied or pushed aside, Anthony encouraged him into karate as a boy, teaching him to defend himself. Through it all, the family's Catholic faith anchored them, helping them endure struggles that might have broken others.

By the time Lewis was carving out his Formula 1 career

in 2007, Stevenage had produced only a handful of famous names: footballer Ashley Young, who had been Lewis's schoolmate, and Albert Campbell, the town's first black mayor. Together they represented the pride of a working-class community rarely in the national spotlight. Journalist Gary Younge captured the moment perfectly: 'Right now, black Stevenage represents 100 per cent of the town's most famous sons.'

Hamilton's early life showed how determination, sacrifice and resilience could propel someone from obscurity into the most glamorous sporting arena in the world. His story was not just personal but emblematic, reflecting the social and cultural shifts of post-war Britain: migration, inequality, race, class and the dream that talent could overcome circumstance.

If Hamilton's rise was defined by scarcity and sacrifice, then Lando Norris's beginnings could hardly have been more different. His story opens in Bristol, where he was born in 1999, but his upbringing took root in Glastonbury, Somerset, amid a family environment that was both prosperous and steeped in competition. His father, Adam Norris, had already built and sold a pensions empire by his mid-thirties, later becoming a major investor in technology and e-mobility start-ups. The Sunday Times Rich List once ranked him among the wealthiest people in Britain. Lando's mother, Cisca, was Belgian, from the Flanders region, and had grown up with sport as a natural part of life. Competition, in fact, ran through the family. Lando's older brother Oliver tried his hand at karting, and his sister Flo would go on to become an international showjumper. It was a household where achievement wasn't unusual but expected.

The young Lando was sent to Millfield, the famous Somerset school that seemed designed for exactly that kind of trajectory. Known for producing Olympians, rugby internationals and tennis stars, Millfield offered not just elite education but also the sort of facilities and coaching infrastructure that few children ever encounter. Norris joined Millfield Prep at the age of seven and quickly began to channel his energy into racing. The environment was not only nurturing but also professionalised. 'I've had a personal trainer and manager since I was twelve,' he admitted in an interview years later, describing the bubble that surrounded him.

He started out on quad bikes and motorbikes before moving into karts, inspired by watching a national event. The family could afford the best equipment, mechanics and travel to European circuits that quickly put him on the map. Still, his trajectory wasn't effortless.

Unlike Hamilton, who often won races on raw determination, Norris spent his first years in karting without much success. 'In my first, like, four years of karting, I won one race,' he confessed. Those early frustrations instilled in him patience, humility and discipline. By 2013, however, his persistence bore fruit: he became the youngest ever karting world champion in Bahrain, having also racked up European and Supercup titles along the way. From then on, his progress was rapid.

McLaren soon spotted his talent and signed him as a junior driver, setting him on the path to Formula 1.

Norris himself was always keenly aware of the privileged environment that had cushioned his rise. 'I never wanted him [my dad] to pay for me to come into Formula 1,' he explained on *The High Performance Podcast* in 2024. 'That was one goal. He could support me until Formula 1, or let's say Formula 2, but I personally wouldn't want to come into Formula 1 having to pay for it. It makes me much prouder to say I'm here because McLaren brought me on.' That desire to prove himself on merit, not simply on resources, became a defining aspect of his character.

Yet he never denied the role his father played in smoothing the path. 'I have to know that to a certain extent I'm lucky for the opportunities that I got, and the fact he could just support me into Formula 2 was already a lot more than what other people get. So, I also know that on the flip side.'

This mixture of self-awareness and gratitude gave Norris a perspective sometimes lacking in other wealthy young athletes. He recognised the safety net beneath him, but he also understood that without talent and results, that safety net could not carry him to Formula 1.

Millfield itself later celebrated his achievements with pride. In 2022, the school awarded him its Old Millfieldian of the Year honour alongside footballer Tyrone Mings, actress Rose Leslie and a professor of experimental medicine, Peter Openshaw. The school's statement described Norris's time there in glowing terms: 'Lando Norris was brought up in Glastonbury and attended Millfield for nine years, joining Millfield Prep School in Year 2 before departing Millfield in Year 10. Lando started kart racing as a pupil at

Millfield Prep School, aged seven. After his first couple of seasons racing in junior single-seater championships, he was placed firmly on the motorsport map.'

By the time Norris made his Formula 1 debut in 2019 at the Australian Grand Prix, he was not only McLaren's youngest driver but also the youngest Brit ever to start a race. His first seasons showed steady progress – 11th in the standings in 2019, ninth the following year with his first podium, and later, sixth with further podiums and even a pole position. In 2022, McLaren extended his contract until 2025, cementing his place as one of the sport's rising stars.

The contrast with Hamilton was apparent. Lewis grew up on a council estate, his father getting cash to help his son via endless overtime.

Lando grew up in a world where money was not a problem.

Hamilton's dad fought to keep racism and poverty from crushing his son's dreams. Norris's father gave him freedom to focus entirely on getting to the very top. Both men were determined, but their struggles were radically different.

Yet there's another side to Lando's story, which proves privilege alone can't buy success in F1. Over the years, many drivers from privileged backgrounds have not achieved the glory that Lando has. Without mental toughness, and an inbuilt ability to handle pressure, Norris could not have done so. McLaren chief Zak Brown put it simply: 'He had pretty much won everything he'd ever sat in at a very young age. That means he's an extremely special talent.'

Norris was no overnight creation of his father's fortune.

He was the product of years of hard graft and progress one race at a time. For all the privilege of his upbringing, he also knew he wouldn't make it unless he gave everything. 'There are a lot of things that my dad has given to me – invested in me,' he said. 'I'll need to pay back that investment and reward him and use what he's given me to show it's all been useful and not a waste of time.' His parents, he added, kept him from becoming big-headed. 'The one thing my mum and dad have done very well, I would say, is keeping me grounded and [teaching me] to live life as normally as possible, and not get carried away in any way.'

If Hamilton's story is one of struggle, and Norris's one of privilege, then George Russell's life falls somewhere in between the two – more towards comfort than struggle, yet far removed from the limitless resources of a billionaire's household.

His path reflects the reality for many families who find themselves trying to propel a son into the pinnacle of motorsport that is F1: not destitute, nor wealthy, but stretched to breaking point by the sheer cost of chasing a dream.

Russell was born in King's Lynn, Norfolk, in 1998, the youngest of three children. His father, Steve, ran a modest business trading seeds, peas and pulses. His mother, Alison, was a hairdresser. The family was close-knit, practical and determined. George grew up alongside his brother, Benjy, himself a talented karter who clinched the 2007 Super 1 National Championship, and his sister, Cara.

It was Benjy who inspired George to race with the number 63, a number that followed him through the junior categories and into Formula 1. Motorsport quickly became a family project. Steve Russell threw himself into supporting George's career, investing huge sums into the boy's karting. Estimates put the eventual figure at around £1.5 million – money that did not come from a trust fund or inherited wealth but, like Lewis's and Lando's dad, painstaking graft.

At first Steve tried to balance the costs with his business, but as George climbed the junior ranks and the bills grew steeper, he made a fateful decision. In 2012, he sold the family firm outright, freeing up capital to keep George's dream alive. It was a risk of staggering proportions: sacrificing a steady livelihood for the uncertain possibility of a child's career in one of the most cut-throat sports in the world.

The family's devotion was total. Steve doubled as mechanic, driver-coach and chief strategist. Alison meticulously recorded lap times, carburettor settings and track conditions, scrawling notes at circuits up and down the country. George later described how every weekend, for years on end, was consumed by racing. 'My father was my mechanic, my driver-coach. My mother wrote down all of these set-ups and the lap times of every single track,' he told *The Times*. 'We weren't wealthy like some F1 drivers. My earliest memories are of living in a mobile home while my parents built a house in a field in the middle of nowhere, near Wisbech in Cambridgeshire.'

What marked Russell's upbringing was that sacrifice by his family, but also a father who demanded he do all in his power to be a success on the track. Steve Russell was a strict, uncompromising figure who urged his son to scale what seemed impossible heights. George recalled that from around the ages of eight to 18, their relationship was defined by tension. 'I never saw my dad Monday to Friday because he was working. He'd leave before I woke up. I was in bed by the time he got back. At weekends, unless we won, the relationship with him was quite tough because he was so hard on me. For probably five to ten years of my life, our relationship wasn't great, but you don't really comprehend why. You don't understand the context. He only wanted the best for me, but if he saw that I wasn't giving it my all, no wonder he was getting stressed and angry at me because he was sacrificing his whole time to give me this opportunity.'

The pressure could be suffocating, but it made George find an inner perfectionism and resilience that would become central to his driving.

Where Norris spoke of gratitude and Hamilton of sheer determination, Russell often framed his success in terms of discipline.

His father's relentless demands hardened him, creating a driver for whom detail, precision and effort became second nature. Even now, as a Mercedes driver, his reputation is not of flamboyance or instinct but of meticulousness and rigour – qualities that trace back to those long weekends under his father's watchful eye.

When George was eight, the family moved to Milton Keynes to be closer to his junior racing team. He left Wisbech Grammar School and later shifted to home schooling, freeing time for his burgeoning career. He lived much of his youth not in grand houses or gated estates, but in caravans and half-built homes, the family making do while pouring resources into his future. It was a childhood marked by single-minded focus, with his family fully behind him every step of the way.

By his teenage years, Steve made it clear that the family's financial contribution had limits. He urged George to seek out a junior driver programme to relieve the burden. 'When I was 16,' George later explained, 'he told me: you have to find a way to make this sustainable.' That push led to George joining Mercedes' junior programme, a crucial step that ensured his path upwards did not collapse for a lack of funding.

In later life, Russell has looked back at those years with gratitude and understanding. 'He moulded me into the guy I am today,' he said of his father.

The strictness, the long silences on weekends when races went badly, the pressure to excel – all of it contributed to the driver he became. What others might have resented, he came to see as part of the necessary sacrifice to reach the top.

In this, his story mirrors Hamilton's more than Norris's. Both Hamilton and Russell grew up knowing that their families were giving everything they had to keep them racing. Both felt the strain of fathers who pushed them, sometimes to breaking point, in the name of maximising their sons' potential.

Norris, by contrast, never carried that same burden. His challenge was different – proving that money had not made him soft, that he could still earn his place at the top table. For Hamilton and Russell, the challenge was enduring the weight of sacrifice, proving worthy of what had been given up for them.

Russell's success has validated his family's gamble. From karting to Formula 3 champion, from Williams to Mercedes, he has built a career marked by professionalism and relentless application. Yet the echoes of those early years remain, visible in the way he carries himself and the way he talks about racing. His father may never have held a trophy, but his fingerprints are all over George's career.

The stories of Hamilton, Norris and Russell reveal not just the making of three outstanding British drivers, but the making of Formula 1 itself.

Behind the glamour of the grid, beyond the roar of engines and the glare of sponsorship lies a truth that is both sobering and fascinating: no one arrives at the summit alone. Every lap completed on Sunday afternoons has been paved by years of family sacrifice or fortune. The drivers are the visible stars, but behind them stand fathers, mothers, grandparents, whole family structures that either bore the weight of financial strain, opened doors with their wealth, or mapped out the future with relentless determination.

Hamilton's journey shows us how rare it is for someone from a modest background to break into this glamorous, rarefied world. His was a story built on the back of a father who worked three jobs, a grandfather who came to Britain in the *Windrush* era, and a childhood spent battling both poverty and prejudice. He embodied what it meant to fight through every barrier, his story both a personal triumph and a social statement.

His success didn't simply add to Formula 1's record books, it rewrote them, forcing the sport to confront questions about race, class and access that had long been ignored. Norris's path, by contrast, illustrates the opposite end of the tale. Born into wealth, educated at elite schools and supported by a family that could bankroll him, his was a career made possible initially by privilege. Yet that privilege would only take him so far. He had to put in the graft himself to justify the more comfortable route offered to him. To prove that talent and dedication mattered as much as money. To make sure his story was not dismissed as one of entitlement but celebrated as one of merit. In his own words, it mattered deeply that he was chosen by McLaren, not just a lucky lad who had been funded by his father. That distinction was crucial as it shaped his sense of pride.

Russell, finally, occupies the middle ground. Not poor, not rich, but stretched thin by the immense costs of junior racing. His father sold the family business to fund his dream, his mother recorded data at every race, and his brother mentored him. Their support was absolute, but it came with pressure. The family gave up stability for his chance, and that gamble created a relationship of both love and strain.

His story is a reminder that Formula 1 careers are rarely just about the driver. They are about whole families bending their lives around one child's ambition, often at enormous cost.

Looked at together, these three lives offer up a portrait of what it takes to reach Formula 1 in the modern era. They show us that there is no single route; that access to motorsport demands either money, sacrifice or inheritance, and usually a combination of all three. In Hamilton's case, it was sacrifice against the odds. In Norris's, it was money that had to be justified by results. In Russell's, it was the sale of security for the hope of a future.

The emotional dynamics, too, differ just as sharply. Hamilton and Russell describe fathers whose expectations could be suffocating, whose sacrifices created a tension that only later softened into gratitude. Norris remembers parents who kept him grounded without the strain of poverty hanging over them. These relationships are central to understanding the men who sit behind the wheel. For all the talk of natural talent and raw speed, it is parenting, background and the invisible scaffolding of family that moulds a driver.

What emerges most clearly is that there is no true meritocracy in this sport. The barriers to entry are too high, the costs too steep, the opportunities too uneven. And yet, within those constraints, something extraordinary still shines through. Because while money or lineage may open doors, they cannot keep a driver there. Results, resilience and talent remain the ultimate currency. Privilege can buy time, but it cannot manufacture wins. Sacrifice can provide opportunity, but it cannot guarantee podiums. Each of our three Brits, in their own way, had to deliver when it mattered.

Perhaps that is why their stories resonate. They remind us that Formula 1 is not only about the speed of cars but about the weight of histories – family histories, national histories, class histories – that come roaring into every corner. Hamilton carries the struggles of working-class Britain and the legacy of Caribbean migration. Norris embodies the comforts of wealth and the burden of proving merit within it. Russell is the son of a small businessman who gambled everything and, against the odds, won.

Together they show us Formula 1's true hinterlands: the invisible terrain of class, family and circumstance that lies behind the glitter of the grid. The sport may present itself as the pinnacle of individual performance, but it is in fact the product of collective sacrifice, advantage and determination. The fathers who worked three jobs, the mothers who scribbled lap times, the billionaires who helped their children arrive – all of them are as much a part of the story as the drivers themselves. Formula 1 is a contest of speed, yes, but also of beginnings.

And so, when the lights go out on Sundays and the cars surge forward, what we are really watching is not just a race between 20 drivers, but a race between histories: the boy from Stevenage whose father worked night and day, the boy from Glastonbury who had every resource at his disposal and the Norfolk lad whose family sold their livelihood for a chance. They all arrive at the same grid, but the roads that brought Lewis, Lando and George to that juncture could not be more different.

CHAPTER 2

ABSOLUTE BEGINNERS

Karting offered the natural initial habitat for our British trio of the modern era as it tends to be for most Formula 1 hopefuls. The sport is not just the first step – it's the defining step. It teaches the fundamentals, reveals character and separates the gifted from the merely ambitious. For Lewis Hamilton, Lando Norris and George Russell, karting was the arena where their destinies began to unfold.

In the world of Formula 1, where precision, reflexes and racecraft define champions, karting is more than a childhood pastime, it's the crucible where elite drivers are forged. Nearly every F1 driver, from legends like Ayrton Senna to modern geniuses like Max Verstappen, began their journey in a kart.

But why is karting so universally regarded as the first essential step towards F1 glory?

Well, Hamilton once succinctly summed it up in this way: 'Karting offers a unique blend of accessibility, intensity and technical challenge that makes it ideal for young drivers.' He also explained that it enabled him to get the feel of racing at a tender age – most children can begin karting as early as age five or six, allowing them to develop race instincts before adolescence. It led to him developing core, and vital, racing skills: braking, cornering, overtaking and defending, which he could use successfully in older age group competitions. It also builds resilience, focus and strategic thinking under pressure.

There is a financial cost with the karts, but it is much less dependent on expensive machinery as is the case further up the racing scale, allowing youngsters to take part even if their families aren't wealthy.

In that sense, karting is the most meritocratic rung on the ladder to F1.

As any would-be Hamilton would tell you, the circuit often attracts scouts from F1 teams and academies to assess the latest raw talent in the karts.

Hamilton has spoken often about his background, starting when his father bought him a radio-controlled car as a five-year-old. When he finished second in a national British Radio Car Association championship the following year, against adult competition, his father instinctively knew he would be a natural in karts.

Lewis began karting seriously at eight after persuading Anthony to procure him a kart. Without significant financial backing, the family relied on second-hand equipment and long weekends spent travelling to races. Anthony Hamilton acted as mechanic, manager and financier, stretching income from his jobs to cover entry fees and running costs.

From such a cash-stretched background, his son's ascent to F1 relied on talent and opportunity colliding at critical junctures. With McLaren's junior programme supporting him from his early teens, he gained financial and technical backing. But until that point, the onus had been on his family to fund every entry fee, tyre purchase and race trip. 'My dad is the reason I'm here. He did everything to make sure I could race,' he admitted. 'We never went on holiday, never had new clothes, but I was always on the grid.'

Norris's junior career unfolded more comfortably given his family's financial advantages. Early access to international karting, test days, spare parts, elite coaching and a supportive family network enabled a seamless ascent through the ranks. The ability to invest time and energy without interruption set the stage for his later dominance in single-seaters. Plus, the Norris household was a broad sporting organism: karting, showjumping, competitive athletics all co-existed, encouraging a culture of performance. The seamless integration of sport into family life provided a normalised context for obsession, discipline and strategic growth.

The Hamilton family, by contrast, was singularly fixated. Motorsport became the sinew of family unity. While Lewis pursued racing, his family suspended other possibilities. Weekend days at the track, evenings planning set-ups, and every available pound was funnelled into the one objective of building a future motor racing star, whatever the financial and personal costs or burdens.

For George Russell, the karting journey began at the age of seven in King's Lynn, Norfolk, inspired by his older brother, Benjy. His karting years were marked by discipline and determination, traits that continue to define his F1 career. He had tried other sports in his youth, but only karting mattered after he got a grip on it. He told *KL Magazine*, 'If you have the opportunity to try out more than one sport that's great. I used to play football when I was a youngster until I learned that go-karting was my passion. The advice I would give to any parent – whether their child wants to be a racing driver or a footballer – is firstly to encourage whatever their passion is.'

He remains indebted to Benjy for the role he played in initially enticing him into a kart. 'Because of my older brother's influence it was natural for me to go into karting from a young age. And I enjoyed it right from the start.' He added, 'My mother and father also supported me a huge amount; it was a real family team effort.'

George began karting in 2006 and swiftly demonstrated natural ability, and by 2009, he had progressed to the cadet class, winning both the MSA British Cadet Championship and the British Open. In 2010, he moved to the Rotax Mini Max category, where he dominated the British karting scene. That year, he won three tournaments: the Super One British Championship, the Formula Kart Stars British Championship and the Kartmasters British Grand Prix.

The victories established him as a rising star. In 2011,

he graduated to the KF3 class and joined the Intrepid Driver Program, racing alongside future F1 drivers Alex Albon and Charles Leclerc. That year, Russell won the CIK-FIA European Championship and the SKUSA SuperNationals title in Las Vegas. The following year, he made history by becoming the first driver to successfully defend the Junior European Championship.

He nearly repeated his SKUSA win, finishing second after Lance Stroll's disqualification was overturned. In 2013, his final karting year, Russell moved to the KF1 category and finished 19th in the CIK-FIA World Championship.

Much later, George would say, 'Karting was everything to me. It taught me the fundamentals of racing and gave me the hunger to succeed.'

Lewis Hamilton first tried a go-kart during a family break in Spain. The experience was enough to hook him, and not long after, his father, Anthony, scraped together about £1,000 to buy one for him. His mother, Carmen, remembered her surprise when the kart arrived just before Lewis's eighth birthday – complete with race suit and helmet. 'He was straight in it,' she recalled, 'heading down the street like he'd been born to do it.' What began with model cars swiftly progressed to karts, and before long, to dreams of Formula 1.

Lewis was similarly mesmerised by the karting world, and F1, even at the age of eight, thanks to his idol, Ayrton Senna. When Senna lost his life at Imola in 1994, Lewis was only nine and competing in a kart race that weekend. The tragedy hit him hard. 'I didn't show it in front of Dad,' Lewis later said. 'I went behind the trailer and cried. It was

21

a turning point; realising heroes aren't invincible made me determined to make the most of my talent.'

At ten, his life took another step forward when dad Anthony brought him to Rye House kart track, just south of Stevenage. He had already shown his pace by out-lapping his father at other circuits, but now Lewis announced he wanted to race professionally. Even as a novice, he was mixing it with the quickest on track. One regular at Rye House, Martin Hines of Zipkart, spotted the youngster immediately. 'With a black plate, most drivers are at the back,' Hines explained. 'But here was this kid fighting at the front. You could see it instantly – he was something else.' Hines offered to supply the Hamiltons with a chassis, beginning a five-year partnership.

That same year, at just ten years old, he became the youngest ever British cadet kart champion. The title earned him a trip to London's Autosport Awards, where he famously approached McLaren team principal Ron Dennis for an autograph and boldly told him he intended to drive for McLaren one day.

Dennis signed his book with the words, 'Phone me in nine years.' In reality, their professional connection would begin only three years later.

Hamilton laughs about that first meeting now. 'We couldn't afford a suit, so I borrowed one from the guy who'd won the championship before me, shoes and all. I went up to Ron and told him I'd be world champion for McLaren. He told me to get in touch in nine years, but a couple or so years later, he called me.'

The karting successes came thick and fast. In 1996, Hamilton won the Champions of the Future, Sky TV KartMasters and the Five Nations titles. Moving into junior Yamaha in 1997, he repeated his Champions of the Future success and added the Super One championship. Former Jaguar Racing boss Tony Purnell, whose Pi Research company sponsored him for a time, believed he was witnessing the future of the sport. 'Since he was 12, with McLaren's backing, he's had the best equipment,' Purnell said. 'But you still need the talent to use it – and Lewis always destroyed his teammates.'

Despite the growing demands of racing, Anthony also ensured Lewis remained focused on education. On the track, though, the winning streak continued. In 1998, racing in Junior Intercontinental A, Hamilton finished second in the McLaren Mercedes Champions of the Future and fourth at the Italian Open.

The following year, he won the Italian Industrials at Intercontinental A level, took the runner-up spot in the European Championship, and claimed the Trophy de Pomposa. He was also placed fourth again at the Italian Open in his category.

The year 2000 was a landmark. Hamilton dominated Formula A, winning all four rounds to take the European Championship. He also captured the World Cup and triumphed at the prestigious Bercy Masters. That season ended with him named the British Racing Drivers' Club's 'Rising Star'.

By then, six years had passed since a pact he and Anthony

had made to reach the top. In that time, Lewis had moved in with his father, given up much of a typical teenager's social life, and focused on nothing but racing.

With every major karting title to his name and McLaren now officially supporting his career through their development programme, Hamilton was ready for the next leap – from karts to cars – and the start of his campaign to conquer the racing world.

For Lando Norris, karting would bring even greater recognition than Hamilton or Russell – in the form of being acclaimed as the youngest ever world champion. He began kart racing aged eight, and in his first national event, secured pole position – a sign of innate speed and composure from the outset.

Lando's progress continued, but he was steady rather than spectacular, from 2010 to 2012. In 2010, he finished 27th in Kartmasters British Grand Prix and tenth in the Formula Kart Stars MSA – Cadet. The low placings continued, with a 27th and 25th spot in early events.

But he finished fifth in the Super 1 National Championship and sixth in the MSA British Championship signalled improvement.

By 2012, he was beginning to shape up, finishing fourth in the Kartmasters GP. He failed to make the podium in events such as the Formula Kart Stars and WSK Final Cup, but felt he was on the brink of a statement win as the races and the valuable experience mounted. The following year, strong results proved that his optimism hadn't been misplaced. In the KF-Junior category, he finished fifth in the South Garda Winter Cup and the Trofeo Andrea Margutti.

Then came the real breakthroughs: champion at the KFIA European Championship, Winner of the KFIA International Super Cup and top of the standings in the WSK Euro Series. No longer was the boy a wannabe, now he was becoming the main character in the drama. That fact was amplified in 2014 when Lando Norris scooped the world karting crown. In doing so at the age of 14, he became the youngest winner of the CIK-FIA KF World Championship, a title he won in his first year of competing in the KF category. The victory was particularly memorable as he took the title from Lewis Hamilton, the previous youngest champion in the category. The baton had been passed on from one great Briton who had already achieved F1 glory, to another who would eventually join him.

McLaren's own website summed up his rise from initial karting struggles to king of all he surveyed in this way: 'Despite spanning the globe, motorsport is a village. Everybody knows everybody else, everybody talks over the back fence, and thus Lando was tapped as one to watch long before he came to public prominence. His karting record was stellar: Formula Kart Stars MiniMax champion in 2012, then 2013 CIK-FIA KFJ European champion, CIK-FIA KFJ International Super Cup champion, WSK Euro Series KFJ champion. In 2014, at the age of 14, he made history by becoming the youngest CIK-FIA KF world champion (taking that particular accolade from Lewis Hamilton).'

The team seemed to take particular delight in noting that Lando had surpassed Lewis in the history books . . .

Asked about surpassing the guy who would become a seven-time F1 world champion, Lando was generous in his praise and admiration, saying, 'I kind of look up to Lewis, not as a hero, but as a very good driver who is very fast.' And he was modest about his own talent: 'I think as long as I do a good job and put all my effort into proving that I'm worth it, then everything should be fine. I am absolutely my own biggest critic.'

In 2019, Lando opened up about his karting days to the RaceBox and told them how it had proved helpful in his development as a person, as well as a racer. He told the website, 'The main thing is that you learn a lot about the initial basics of a lot of things: the racecraft, how to put a qualifying lap together, a lot of the baselines for a lot of things you need, not just for Formula 1 but car racing. Although it's still very different [in F1], all of the characteristics are kind of similar.

'Karting was nice because it was more relaxed, in a way, and a lot more open. You can have a lot more of a jolly than you can in F1. You go and drive, do the race and, as soon as you finish, it's like you're in school during break time; you go and have fun. Generally, you also have a lot more teammates, friends and mates around; it's more social. This is something I do in F1 but it's more restricted.'

Then, in an interview with the *Beyond the Grid* podcast, he elaborated further, explaining that it wasn't just 'more fun', but that there were stresses, too, that he had to learn to deal with. He said, 'Karting was about driving and testing on Wednesday and Thursday, then racing on Friday, Saturday and Sunday. It was like that for the majority of the weeks, at least two every month in Italy, Spain, the UK. I was travelling from Tuesday evening or sometimes from Tuesday at lunch [until Sunday]. It was a lot of time.

'I don't know why anyone would cope with the idea of having Wednesday to Thursday to Friday to Saturday to Sunday, weeks of karting. I was doing it when I was 12, 13 years old, but there are kids who do that on a regular basis at eight or nine years old. It was a bad thought process from whoever came out with that – but now they've changed it to usually Friday, Saturday and Sunday.'

Two Brit legends from earlier eras also set the pace in the karting world, and both also went on to become major names in F1: Jenson Button and David Coulthard.

Button started karting around the age of eight in 1988, after receiving a Zip go-kart as a Christmas present and debuting at Clay Pigeon Raceway. He enjoyed much more early age success than Norris, scooping the British Super Prix aged nine, and was undefeated in the 1991 British Cadet Kart Championship, winning all 34 races.

Jenson also had success in more elite international karting events – which often pit youngsters against future Formula 1 drivers. The progression from Formula A to Super A marks a transition from top-tier youth karting to professional-level karting, just before stepping into single-seaters and Jenson proved he was worthy of a spot.

He was runner-up in the Formula A World Championship aged 15, fifth in the 1996 European Formula A Championship and third in both the Formula A World Cup and the American Championship. The following year, he won the Ayrton Senna Memorial Cup, became the youngest driver and first Briton to win the European Super A Championship, and was runner-up in the Winter Cup.

David Coulthard was another karting success story. The Scottish ace began karting aged 11 and had direct motivation and inspiration to succeed from within his family. His father was a Scottish karting campaigner and kart champion, which gave David early exposure to the sport.

He went on to win several local Scottish championships, including the Scottish Junior Kart Championship and the Scottish Kart Championship. David also triumphed in the Cumbria Kart Racing Club Championship. As with our previously noted British karters, it led him to F1. In 1989, he transitioned into car racing, ultimately becoming the inaugural winner of the McLaren Autosport Young Driver of the Year Award.

It all goes to show that karting success has long been the proving ground for aspiring British Formula 1 drivers, and over the years it has solidified its reputation as the most effective and essential route to the pinnacle of motorsport. From the grassroots level to international championships, it teaches the fundamentals of racecraft, vehicle control and competitive instinct that are indispensable in Formula 1. The careers of Lewis Hamilton, Lando Norris, George Russell, David Coulthard and Jenson Button all began in karting, and their trajectories underscore its value as a launch pad for elite racing talent.

But the shift to karting as a universal entry point to Formula 1 is a relatively modern phenomenon. In earlier decades, fellow Brit drivers like John Surtees came from different backgrounds – in John's case, motorcycle racing. Surtees became the only person to win world championships on both two and four wheels, by winning seven bike world championships with MV Agusta before switching to Formula 1 in 1960 and winning one F1 World Championship.

Fellow Brit and former F1 champion Damon Hill also avoided the karting route into F1. Like Surtees, he arrived after racing motorbikes.

However, karting is by far the most common pathway and is a worthwhile proving ground for aspiring F1 drivers, as our modern era Brit karting winners gladly testify.

CHAPTER 3

ON THE SHOULDERS OF GIANTS

Hamilton, Norris and Russell are but the latest diamonds to shine in what is a storied lineage of British motor racing legends. The trio encompass the present and future, although in Hamilton's case more a glorious past, but all three agree they have been inspired and motivated by the exploits of a series of brilliant UK drivers from more distant eras.

Jim Clark, one of the most naturally gifted drivers in F1 history, came from Scottish farming stock. Born on 4 March 1936 at Kilmany House Farm in Fife, he was the youngest of five and the only boy in his family. Jim spent his youth amid sheep and acres of farmland, a far cry from roaring engines and chequered flags.

When he was six, his family relocated to Edington Mains Farm near Chirnside in the Scottish Borders, where Clark's early schooling in local livestock-rich communities gave way to a mechanical curiosity that charted his destiny. Though his parents bristled at the distractions of motorsport, Clark began rallying his own Sunbeam Talbot in hill-climb events, displaying raw car control and courage well beyond expectations.

By 1958, racing for the Border Reivers team in Jaguars and Porsches, he won 18 races, which was enough to catch the eye of Lotus founder Colin Chapman. He swiftly graduated from Formula Junior to F2, and then F1 by the end of 1960.

Jim showed his remarkable skills in all weathers at Spa in 1963. It was a rain-soaked Belgian Grand Prix where he started eighth, navigated fog and a jammed fifth gear to lap all but one rival, winning by nearly five minutes. He would go on to win his first F1 world title later that season.

In 1965, he won seven of ten races, clinching his second title with three rounds left – and becoming the only driver to win multiple championships, including F1, Tasman, French and British F2, all in the same year.

His Indy 500 victory that year, in a rear-engined Lotus as he led for 150 of 200 laps, helped revolutionise American open-wheel design. Clark's command of machinery inspired Jackie Stewart to call him 'so smooth . . . he sort of caressed [the car] into doing what he wanted', and another all-time great, Juan Manuel Fangio, described Clark as the greatest driver ever. Jackie Stewart also said Jim was the most complete racer he ever saw.

Tragically, Jim's life and career were cut short when he died in a Formula 2 crash at Hockenheim in April 1968, aged 32. His Lotus-Cosworth skidded off the track and somersaulted into a wood at 170mph. He had won 25 Grands Prix and notched 33 pole positions. His legacy lives on through the Jim Clark Trust and thousands of people have visited the Jim Clark Motorsport Museum since it opened to the public in 2019.

In modern terms, Lewis Hamilton's mantle of dominance echoes Clark's journey. If Clark was a craftsman of pure precision, Sir Stirling Moss was racing's suavely articulate artist. Born 17 September 1929 in Kensington, west London, Moss was a scion of motorsport. His father Alfred raced in the 1924 Indy 500 and his mother in pre-war hill climbs. Young Stirling alternated between equestrian competitions and mechanical tinkering, the winnings from the former funding his purchase of a Cooper 500 at just 15 – a seed for his meteoric ascent.

Beginning with dominant success in F3 in 1948, he claimed the RAC Tourist Trophy, Mille Miglia, Sebring and many more, driving an astonishing array of machinery, often proudly British.

'It is better to lose honourably in a British car than to win in a foreign one,' he said, embodying both patriotism and sportsmanship. Moss never won a world title, despite 16 F1 wins and four consecutive runner-up championship finishes. He achieved a world record 212 wins across various motorsport disciplines, including Grand Prix, sports cars and rallying.

In 1958, Moss missed out on becoming the first British driver to win the F1 world title but showed he was the ultimate sportsman. The *Scotsman* newspaper summed up how in a wonderful obituary when he died aged 90 in 2020. It read: 'Moss's championship rival Mike Hawthorn was set to be excluded from the Portuguese Grand Prix after a marshal claimed he had illegally rejoined the track following a spin. Hawthorn's disqualification would have seen Moss crowned champion.

'But Moss, who had dominated the race to win by more than five minutes, jumped to his rival's defence and rubbished the marshal's claim. Hawthorn was reinstated to second and Moss, despite winning four races to his rival's one, would miss out on glory by a single point.'

Moss recalled the gesture years later in typically modest style, 'I had no hesitation in doing it. I can't see how this is open to debate. The fact that he was my only rival in the championship didn't come into my thinking. Absolutely not.'

His career ended on Easter Monday 1962 when he was cut out of his car following a 100mph crash at Goodwood. He was knighted in 2000.

His class and adaptability bring to mind how Lewis Hamilton has consistently presented himself on and off the track. Similarly, how both men raised the profile of the sport via their genuine sportsmanship. On the legend's 90th, Lewis praised him, saying, 'Stirling is a great ambassador for the sport and the UK.'

Meanwhile, Stirling once said, 'I hope I'll continue to be described as the greatest driver who never won the World Championship, but it doesn't really matter. The most important thing for me was gaining the respect of the other drivers and I think I achieved that.' No doubt whatsoever about that, Sir Stirling.

Sir Jackie Stewart also contributed massively to the sport in a specific way – via his insistence on improving safety standards. He revolutionised attitudes towards driver safety, pushing for proper barriers, run-off areas and medical facilities. Known as 'the Flying Scot', he was respected for saving lives, but also the speeds he notched up on the track. In his era, he was also a giant of F1, a triple world champion in 1969, 1971 and 1973.

Born in Dumbarton, Scotland, in 1939 to garage-owning parents, Jackie left school at 15 due to dyslexia. Instead, he worked as an apprentice in his father's garage business, where his mechanical intuition began to flourish. He was also an exceptional sportsman in his youth, representing Scotland in clay-pigeon shooting and winning multiple championships before ever stepping into a racing car. His break in racing came almost by chance. Barry Filer, a customer at the family garage, convinced Stewart to test some of his cars, and he was spotted by Ken Tyrrell, leader of the Formula Junior team.

Tyrrell offered him a place on the team after watching him beat experienced F1 driver Bruce McLaren's lap times in the Cooper F3.

Stewart's Formula 1 debut in 1965 with BRM quickly marked him as a prodigy; that same year he claimed his first Grand Prix win at Monza. His championship campaigns came with Matra in 1969, Tyrrell in 1971 and again in 1973 –

seasons defined by his unmatched consistency and ability to adapt to vastly different car designs and engineering philosophies.

In his 1969 title year, he won six of 11 races, often by commanding margins. In 1971, he took another six wins from 11 starts, mastering circuits from Monaco to the Nürburgring. His third and final title in 1973 was perhaps his most impressive, achieved while competing against a new generation of fast, aggressive drivers, and he sealed it with races to spare.

He retired after winning his last Championship. His total of 27 wins was not equalled for 20 years.

But Stewart's legacy is not solely written in wins and points. His horrifying crash at Spa in 1966 – where he was trapped in his fuel-soaked car for 25 minutes – ignited his crusade for safety. A storm and severe rain led to a seven-driver pile-up on the first lap. Jackie was trapped, but Graham Hill stopped to help him and Stewart escaped before the car caught fire. Stewart remembered it like this, 'At the Belgium Grand Prix in 1966, conditions were bad. There was a river across the track, maybe 2 metres wide, and I aquaplaned. I spun all the way down and off the road, knocked down a woodcutter's hut, knocked down a telegraph pole and went through a fence before dropping down on to the outside basement of a farmhouse, miraculously the right way up.'

At the time, drivers had no seat belts, marshals had no protective gear, and medical facilities were minimal. Stewart lobbied for guard rails, better run-off areas, full-face helmets, fireproof overalls and the formation of a professional driver safety body. He risked unpopularity with organisers by boycotting races at unsafe circuits like Spa and the old Nürburgring.

But his decision saved lives and laid the foundation for the modern safety culture that drivers like Hamilton, Norris and Russell now race within.

Hamilton's own advocacy for diversity and sustainability echoes Jackie's courage in using his position to challenge the sport's status quo. Where Stewart pushed the paddock to value the safety of its drivers as the most important issue, Hamilton continues to push for the sport to reflect inclusivity. Stewart acknowledged this continuity, once remarking of Hamilton, 'What he's done for Britain in motorsport is incredible. He's an exceptional talent and he's using his voice to make changes – much like we had to do for safety.'

Stewart retired at the end of the 1973 season, deciding before the year began that it would be his last. His retirement actually proved to be a race earlier than planned after tragedy struck. His Tyrrell teammate François Cevert was killed in practice for the United States GP, and Stewart, who had already secured the championship, withdrew from what would have been his 100th Grand Prix start. His legacy on the track was 27 victories from 99 starts, making him the most successful driver in F1 history at the time. That record stood for 14 years.

Even after retirement, Stewart retained a strong bond with F1. In 1997, he entered his own race outfit – Stewart Racing Team – which was later sold to Jaguar. In 2005,

Red Bull Racing emerged from the Jaguar team, giving the brilliant Scot a link to today's heroes of the track, including the volatile genius Max Verstappen.

Graham Hill, the silver-tongued aristocrat of Formula 1, was born on 15 February 1929 in Hampstead, north-west London, to a comfortable middle-class family. His father was a stockbroker and his mother a silverware designer, ensuring that Hill grew up with polish, education and an instinct for presentation that would later become his trademark. He attended Hendon Technical College and dabbled in engineering before completing his national service as a Royal Navy engine-room artificer, where he learned the mechanical discipline that would serve him well on the track. Remarkably, Hill didn't learn to drive until he was 24, discovering motor racing almost by accident when he took a job at a driving school.

Once bitten by the racing bug, his rise was rapid but hard-fought. He started as a mechanic for Lotus before persuading Colin Chapman to let him test their cars. By 1958, Hill had earned a place on the Lotus F1 team, and by 1962, driving for BRM, he had clinched his first World Championship, defeating Jim Clark. His style was a blend of calculated aggression and smooth, almost theatrical showmanship, qualities that made race fans adore him. His five victories at the Monaco Grand Prix earned him the nickname 'Mr. Monaco', wins that remains unmatched by any British driver.

Ayrton Senna holds the absolute record for victories in Monaco with six wins. He triumphed first in 1987 and then consecutively from 1989 to 1993. His ease and mastery on the winding track of the Principality earned him the nickname 'King of Monaco' – one stage up from our Graham!

Graham's second world title came in 1968 with Lotus in the shadow of tragedy after the death of teammate and friend Jim Clark earlier that season. His ability to carry the team's hopes through grief and still deliver consistent performances spoke volumes about his resilience and leadership.

Beyond Formula 1, Hill's ambitions reached further. In 1966, he won the Indianapolis 500, adapting to oval racing's unique demands with consummate ease, such were his racing and driving skills. In 1972, he claimed victory at the Le Mans 24-hour race. The three triumphs – the Monaco GP (and F1 World Championship), Indy 500 and Le Mans – secured him the Triple Crown of Motorsport, a feat no other driver in history has matched.

This versatility mirrors in the modern era George Russell's own adaptability in different conditions and circuits, though Russell is miles apart in terms of titles glory. Hill owned a special blend of technical skill, adaptability and charismatic leadership. Russell's polished public persona, calm under pressure and precision-fuelled driving feel almost like a subtle homage to 'Mr. Monaco' himself, even if separated by decades and vastly different eras of Formula 1.

Hill's later years in racing were spent running his own team, Embassy Hill, and he also appeared on TV in the 1970s on a variety of non-sporting programmes including panel games. But his life was tragically cut short on 29 November 1975 when the plane he was piloting crashed in heavy fog near Arkley golf course, north London. Hill, fellow British racing driver Tony Brise and four other members of Hill's racing team were returning from car testing at Circuit Paul Ricard in France and were due to land at Elstree Airfield. All six were killed.

His death, at just 46, was a devastating blow to British motorsport. Hill's record of 176 Grand Prix starts remained in place for over a decade until being equalled by Jacques Laffite. Damon Hill, Graham's son, was only 15 at the time of his father's death, but his World Championship in 1996 confirmed the continuing power of the Hill name in F1.

And so on to an altogether polar opposite character, and yet still legendary and much loved and missed, British hero of F1. James Hunt, born on 29 August 1947 in Belmont, Surrey, couldn't have been more different from Graham Hill, on and off the track. While Hill was studious and conscientious and careful, Hunt could be unpredictable, irresponsible and daring. He was certainly an unconventional racer who liked a cigarette and a beer and wore 'sex – the breakfast of champions' badges on his overalls.

Hunt came from a comfortable middle-class background. His father was a stockbroker and the young Hunt was sent to well-regarded schools, including Wellington College, where his rebellious streak was already evident. He initially pursued tennis and cricket, and was undoubtedly talented at both, but by his late teens his attention had shifted to motorsport. It was an unusual transition for someone with no mechanical background and it began with a Mini he bought for £50, which he modified and raced in club events.

Hunt's early racing career in Formula Ford and Formula 3 was colourful, erratic and punctuated by spectacular accidents. He earned the nickname 'Hunt the Shunt' for his frequent crashes, yet his speed and charisma made him a crowd favourite. It was during his Formula 3 days that he came under the wing of the flamboyant peer Alexander Hesketh, a rotund young aristocrat determined to bring style, fun and excess to motorsport.

Lord Hesketh's privately funded team became infamous for its champagne-fuelled race weekends, lavish hospitality and devil-may-care approach to competition. Their base was an English country estate, their arrival at races was often in Rolls-Royces or private helicopters, and their philosophy was unapologetically about pleasure as much as performance. It was a dream team for Hunt, as if fatefully created for him, who was known in some circles as a playboy with a happy-go-lucky attitude.

The partnership surprised many pundits on the circuit as Hunt and Hesketh proved the naysayers who had written them off wrong. In 1973, Hunt made his Formula 1 debut with Hesketh Racing, scoring a podium in only his second season and taking the team's only F1 victory at the 1975 Dutch Grand Prix. That win established Hunt as one of the sport's most exciting prospects, and when Emerson Fittipaldi unexpectedly left McLaren at the end of 1975 to start his own team, Hunt was drafted in as his replacement – a move that would define both his career and the 1976 season.

The 1976 Formula 1 Championship remains one of

the most dramatic in racing history, pitting Hunt against the methodical Austrian, Niki Lauda.

The rivalry moved F1 off the back pages on to the tabloid front pages due to Hunt's off-track exploits. The pair's rivalry was fierce but grounded in mutual respect, and off track they were unlikely friends, even flatmates at one stage.

The season began controversially when Hunt was disqualified from a win in Spain only to have it reinstated on appeal. Then came the pivotal moment: at the Nürburgring in August, Lauda suffered a horrific crash that left him with severe burns and lung damage. Remarkably, he returned just six weeks later, but Hunt, seizing momentum, clawed back points through a series of wins.

One of the defining flashpoints came at the 1976 British Grand Prix. The Ferraris collided on the first lap and Hunt's McLaren was damaged in the ensuing debacle. Hunt won the restarted race but was disqualified for failing to complete the first lap of the original race and therefore being ineligible for the restart.

The drama between the duo reached its climax at the season finale in Fuji, Japan. In torrential rain, Lauda withdrew after two laps, declaring the conditions too dangerous. Ferrari had told him they'd camouflage his reasons for opting out, saying it was the engine, but Niki declined.

'Life,' he said, 'is more important than the World Championship.'

Hunt pushed on, finishing third to clinch the championship by a single point, 89 to 88. Lauda later said, 'We were big rivals . . . but I respected him because you could drive next to him – 2 centimetres, wheel by wheel, for 300 kilometres . . . nothing would happen.' Hunt's World Championship catapulted him into global celebrity status, and his playboy lifestyle became as famous as his racing. He was a regular on the London party circuit, linked romantically with models and actresses, and unapologetic about his indulgences.

He chain-smoked, drank heavily and sometimes turned up to races hung-over – yet could still summon electrifying performances.

By 1979, Hunt's appetite for F1 had waned, and after a brief spell with Wolf Racing, he retired at just 31. He moved into broadcasting, becoming a charismatic and often brutally honest BBC commentator alongside Murray Walker, his wit and bluntness making him a fan favourite.

Tragically, Hunt's life was cut short on 15 June 1993 when he died of a heart attack at his Wimbledon home in south-west London at the age of 45. His sudden death shocked the racing world, which remembered him not just as the 1976 champion but as a man who brought glamour, irreverence and sheer joy to a sport that often took itself too seriously. Nowadays, some of Hunt's spirit can be glimpsed in Lando Norris – though Norris's humour and charm are delivered in a social media-savvy, self-aware package rather than Hunt's rock-and-roll recklessness.

Norris's willingness to show vulnerability, admit mistakes and connect with fans echoes the emotional accessibility that made Hunt so beloved. While their eras and temperaments differ, both stand out for injecting personality into the often cosseted world of Formula 1.

While Hunt seemed to emerge from nowhere, Damon Hill, born on 17 September 1960 in Hampstead, London, carried perhaps the heaviest surname in British motorsport. His father, Graham, was already a two-time world champion and one of the sport's most recognisable personalities. Damon's early childhood was marked by privilege, but tragedy struck in 1975 when Graham died in that plane crash.

Damon, then just 15, saw his family's financial security vanish almost overnight. To help make ends meet, he worked a series of manual jobs, including as a motorcycle courier, while completing his education.

His racing career began on two wheels in motorcycle racing before switching to cars in Formula Ford. Though he lacked the early sponsorship and high-profile junior-team backing that many peers enjoyed, his steady progression through Formula 3 and Formula 3000 was built on determination and clean, calculated driving.

Having started his Formula 1 career with the ailing Brabham team, Hill transitioned from Williams test driver to race driver for 1993, after Nigel Mansell exited for IndyCar.

Three years later, he won the 1996 Drivers' Championship, with 21 of his 22 Grand Prix victories coming as a Williams driver. But, in an interview with the *Guardian*, Damon admitted that one of his toughest tasks was to chat with the team's co-founder and boss, Sir Frank Williams.

'I could never have a conversation with Frank,' Hill revealed. 'People used to say they'd spoken to Frank and it was all lovely and I'd go, "Honestly?" I couldn't get two words out of him and it would dry up and he'd stare at his tea. I'd say: "Do you want me to go now?"'

Alain Prost had returned from retirement to lead the team in 1993 but retired again at the end of that campaign after winning the world title. Hill had won three races and finished third overall. For 1994, Ayrton Senna became the new team leader but was killed in his third race with Williams, at Imola. Hill became the de facto team leader. However, his 1994 championship battle with Benetton's Michael Schumacher ended when they collided controversially in the final race at Adelaide. Schumacher, who was accused of taking his rival out, won the title by a single point from Hill.

But Hill got his revenge two years later. Driving the dominant Williams FW18, he won eight of 16 races, sealing the championship at Suzuka and becoming the first son of a world champion to win the title. His victory was as much emotional closure as it was sporting triumph, a redemption arc from the trauma of his father's loss two decades earlier. He was surprisingly, and cruelly, sacked by Williams after scooping the crown. But he remained dignified and composed, refusing to attack Sir Frank. The website F175 summed up the scene: 'Though shocked by his unceremonious dismissal Damon maintained the decorum he thought a champion should have, leaving his indignant wife Georgie (they married in 1988 and had three children) to speak up for him. "Damon has proved himself to have more integrity and dignity in his little finger," Georgie Hill said, "than most people have in their whole body."'

Hill's later career included an unexpected stint with

the struggling Arrows team in 1997, where he nearly won the Hungarian Grand Prix, and a final win for Jordan at the 1998 Belgian Grand Prix – the team's first-ever victory.

After retiring at the end of 1999, he moved into television commentary, became president of the British Racing Drivers' Club, and played a key role in securing the future of the British Grand Prix at Silverstone. His poise under pressure and resilience in the face of adversity mirror how Lewis Hamilton and George Russell have coped with setbacks – refusing to buckle, staying strong and simply getting on with it. Admirable and resilient qualities.

Meanwhile, Nigel Mansell's journey to Formula 1 is one of the most compelling stories of grit and determination in motorsport history. Born on 8 August 1953, in Upton-upon-Severn, Worcestershire, Mansell was raised in Hall Green, Birmingham, where his parents, Eric and Joyce Mansell, ran a modest tea shop. His early life was far removed from the glamour of Formula 1, but it was marked by a fierce ambition that would eventually propel him to the top of the racing world.

Inspired at a young age by watching Jim Clark win the 1962 British Grand Prix, Mansell became obsessed with the idea of becoming a racing driver. Despite limited financial resources, he pursued karting and later moved into Formula Ford, often against his father's wishes. His early racing career was funded almost entirely by personal sacrifice. He sold most of his belongings, quit his job as an aerospace engineer and even remortgaged his home to finance his move into Formula 3.

His wife, Rosanne, stood by him through these difficult decisions, and together they risked everything for his dream. This level of commitment was rare – more recently, George Russell's father Steve took similar risks, as we have noted – and it set Mansell apart from many of his contemporaries. As Formula 1's official Hall of Fame notes, 'No driver fought harder to get into Formula 1 racing and few fought harder when they got there.'

Mansell's path was not without physical hardship. In 1977, while competing in Formula Ford, he suffered a broken neck in a qualifying accident at Brands Hatch. Doctors warned him he was close to paralysis and would never race again. Defying medical advice, Mansell discharged himself from the hospital and returned to racing within weeks. This act of defiance became emblematic of his career – he was a man who refused to be told what he couldn't do.

His break into Formula 1 came in 1980 when Lotus boss Colin Chapman offered him a test drive. Despite suffering burns from a fuel leak during his debut at the Austrian Grand Prix, Mansell impressed enough to earn a full-time seat. Chapman became a mentor and Mansell's loyalty to Lotus was unwavering, even after Chapman's death in 1982. He stayed with the team until 1984 before moving to Williams, where he would eventually win the World Championship in 1992.

Known early on for his fearless overtakes and uncompromising style, Mansell earned the nickname 'Il Leone' (The Lion) from Italian fans for his aggressive drives at Ferrari in the late eighties. But it is the 1992 season that defines his racing career. Mansell won nine of 16 races, took 14 pole positions and secured the championship with five races still to run. Williams's Adrian Newey-designed car with active suspension, semi-automatic gearbox and advanced aero-dynamics has often been described as one of the most technologically advanced F1 cars ever built.

Perhaps his most famous near-miss came at the 1992 Monaco Grand Prix. Leading comfortably, Mansell was forced into a late pit stop after a loose wheel nut was discovered. Rejoining behind Ayrton Senna with just eight laps to go, he launched a relentless pursuit, filling Senna's mirrors and probing every corner for a gap.

'Ayrton could block like a double-decker bus,' he later said, but despite relentless pressure, he could not force a pass. It remains one of the most celebrated duels in F1 history, emblematic of both men's never-say-die mentality.

Mansell's career was also defined by his willingness to take risks beyond F1. After leaving Williams in 1992, he joined IndyCar in the United States and, in his debut season, won the 1993 CART IndyCar World Series Championship, becoming the only person to hold the F1 and IndyCar titles simultaneously.

His later return to F1 was less successful, but his legend had already been cemented. Mansell retired with 31 Grand Prix victories, making him Britain's most successful driver in that context until Hamilton surpassed the mark in 2014. The raw passion, the willingness to wring every last drop from the car and the physical courage in the face of injury are qualities that find a quieter but clear reflection in modern-day hero George Russell's calculated aggression and resilience during high-pressure moments.

Mansell's story is a testament to the power of perseverance. He didn't enter Formula 1 through sponsorship deals or family wealth. Like Lewis Hamilton, he clawed his way in through sheer will. His decision to remortgage his home wasn't just financial – it was symbolic of his total commitment to racing. As Patrick Head of Williams once said, 'Nigel thinks everybody is trying to shaft him at all times' – a reflection perhaps of the motivation that fuelled his relentless drive. That drive made him a champion, and his journey remains one of the most inspiring in Formula 1 history.

Nowadays, Mansell is enjoying his retirement in the Isle of Man and has many businesses and successful enterprises. In September 2023, he decided to let his fans have the chance of owning a piece of racing history by putting his 'hugely personal' memorabilia up for auction for £1.6 million.

It included 32 racing helmets, 78 baseball caps, 50 race suits and more than 200 trophies and awards.

Speaking about the auction, he said, 'It represents the entirety of my career and is the vast majority of the items of clothing I have worn during my racing career: the helmets, suits and all the trophies I have won during more than 30 years of top-flight motorsport.

'It is, in short, the material manifestation of the most significant moments of my career and it represents everything that I worked for from my teenage years through to the end of my racing career.' And boy, did he work hard for it all;

his legacy after that graft – the 1992 World Championship title – is proof enough of that.

Another determined racer was David Coulthard, but much more a 'steady Eddie' than most guys on the F1 circuit. The Scot was known for being a reliable team player – particularly at McLaren, where he often played a supporting role to Mika Häkkinen. He wasn't prone to emotional outbursts or controversial behaviour, and his interviews reflected a thoughtful, measured tone. Even in high-pressure situations, he maintained a calm demeanour, which earned him trust from his engineers and team principals. Engineers trusted his feedback because it was measured and insightful. Coulthard wasn't just fast, he was cerebral, often playing the long game in races and development. An asset to any team, for sure.

Born on 27 March 1971 in Twynholm, Dumfries and Galloway, he grew up in a close-knit Scottish farming and haulage community. David's father, Duncan, was a Scottish karting champion before taking over the family haulage firm, Hayton Coulthard Transport Ltd. His mother, Elizabeth, provided steady emotional support, though she was often nervous about his racing.

Coulthard received his first kart from his father on his 11th birthday, which marked the beginning of his racing journey. He quickly rose through the ranks of British karting and car racing, eventually becoming the first recipient of the McLaren Autosport Young Driver of the Year Award in 1989 – a key milestone that led to his Formula 1 debut.

By his late teens, he had graduated to Formula Ford,

claiming the 1989 British Championship, and then to Formula 3, where he won the 1991 Macau Grand Prix. Coulthard's F1 debut came at the 1994 Spanish Grand Prix, stepping in for Ayrton Senna, who had died at Imola earlier that season. He was Williams's test driver at the time and shared the seat with Nigel Mansell, who returned for select races due to his IndyCar commitments. Coulthard showed maturity and promise, scoring 14 points and finishing eighth in the Drivers' Championship in his debut season.

He also contributed to Williams winning the Constructors' Championship in his debut campaign.

Known for his consistency, technical feedback and willingness to play a supporting role when the team's strategy required it, Coulthard developed a reputation as a consummate professional.

He joined McLaren in 1996 and raced with them for nine seasons, until the end of 2004. He won 12 of his 13 career Grand Prix victories with the team. His best season came in 2001 when he finished runner-up in the World Championship behind Michael Schumacher, scoring 65 points to Schumacher's 123.

David also provided a vital supporting role in McLaren's success during the late 1990s and early 2000s, helping them win the 1998 Constructors' Championship alongside teammate Mika Häkkinen.

Among his most memorable performances was the 2000 French Grand Prix at Magny-Cours, where he overtook Michael Schumacher on track and gave a cheeky hand gesture to the German after being blocked aggressively. His win in Monaco that year also cemented his status as a big-race driver, able to master the sport's most challenging circuits. Even after leaving McLaren for Red Bull in 2005, he played a pivotal role in shaping the then-fledgling team, mentoring a young Sebastian Vettel and helping develop the car into a future championship contender.

He also delivered Red Bull's first-ever podium at Monaco in 2006, proving he still had the edge.

Coulthard retired from Formula 1 at the end of 2008 with 13 career wins, 62 podium finishes and the respect of peers for his professionalism and sportsmanship.

Post-F1, he transitioned seamlessly into broadcasting, becoming a much-respected TV pundit, where his experience from being a driver provided excellent personal and technical analysis for fans.

His career resonates with George Russell's in their shared combination of consistency, adaptability and a calm, pragmatic approach to the pressures of Formula 1. Where Coulthard was the reliable anchor for McLaren and later Red Bull, Russell shows similar traits at Mercedes – quick, disciplined and able to think beyond the next lap. Coulthard never won the world title, but Jenson Button did in 2009, much to the surprise of some pundits and fans. That was because prior to then, he had spent years in underperforming cars, especially during his time with Honda. Despite being seen as technically gifted, he was often labelled a 'nearly man' who would never fulfil his undoubted potential. More echoes of George Russell at

Williams and now Mercedes? Especially in 2024 and 2025 as the latter battled long and hard to get the car up to speed to compete with McLaren.

Born on 19 January 1980 in Frome, Somerset, Jenson was the son of John Button, a former rallycross driver and mechanic, and Simone Lyons.

Button's early years were steeped in motorsport; his father built him his first kart at the age of eight, cobbled together from spare parts and scrap metal, painted in the now-iconic 'Pink Panther' livery. Jenson's natural smoothness behind the wheel was apparent from the start, and he dominated the British karting scene through the early '90s, winning multiple national titles before moving into single-seaters. By 1998, he had taken the British Formula Ford Championship and the prestigious Formula Ford Festival at Brands Hatch, feats that placed him firmly on the radar of Formula 1 scouts.

Button made his F1 debut in 2000 with Williams at just 20 years old, becoming the youngest Briton ever to start a Grand Prix at the time – although, of course, Lando Norris would take that historic record off him.

His early career was marked by flashes of speed, but also the instability of moving between teams – Benetton, Renault, BAR-Honda – as he sought the right environment to flourish. His reputation grew as a master of changing conditions and a driver with an almost uncanny mechanical sympathy, preserving tyres and coaxing cars into performance that seemed beyond their capabilities.

His championship year, 2009, stands as one of the sport's

most remarkable stories. After Honda's withdrawal from F1 in late 2008, Button's career appeared in jeopardy until Ross Brawn led a management buyout, forming Brawn GP. The team arrived at the opening round in Australia with the double-diffuser aerodynamic innovation – a loophole in the regulations – and a car that stunned with its pace. Button seized the opportunity calmly, winning six of the first seven races, including dominant drives in Australia, Malaysia, Bahrain, Spain, Monaco and Turkey.

But it proved more difficult as rivals caught up in development. Fortunately, Button's early points cushion allowed him to adapt his approach. He took a more conservative, points-gathering style in the second half of the season, refusing to be drawn into risks and consistently finishing in the top five. The championship climax came at the Brazilian Grand Prix where Button, starting from 14th, with skilful overtaking managed to finish fifth. It meant he had secured the title with one race to spare. Ecstatic, he sang over the team radio, 'We are the champions!'

Button's 2009 triumph was as much about temperament as raw pace. His smooth, patient style, combined with the ability to read races and adapt strategies mid-race, meant he could extract maximum performance without unnecessary drama. This mental composure, paired with a personable, laid-back nature off the track, made him one of the most popular drivers of his generation. In an era of increasingly corporate F1, Button retained a human warmth, often seen joking with rival drivers in the paddock or calmly handling high-pressure media scrutiny.

His easy-going, laid-back persona brings to mind Lando Norris from our current elite British trio. Both have a relaxed, affable public image. Button was famously smooth and diplomatic; Norris is cheeky and approachable, especially on social media. There's a similarity on the tarmac, too. Button was often lauded for his smooth throttle application, especially in wet conditions. Norris shares this trait – analysts like Peter Windsor have confirmed Norris's style is 'very similar' to Button's, with precise inputs and excellent tyre management.

Speaking on his own YouTube stream in 2023, former Ferrari UK and Williams team manager Windsor said of Button, 'He was very smooth, very, very smooth. Like [Sergio] Perez, incredibly good with power application and in traction episodes; when it was important to get the power down smoothly and well and look after the rear tyres, Jenson was brilliant.

'As I understood it, and you can certainly hear it on the track, there was nobody better than Jenson when it came to the perfection of throttle movement against the brake. He had virtually no overlap unless he wanted to create the overlap – brake against throttle – he was absolutely perfectly synchronised with his feet. Incredible footwork. I think that's one of the reasons he was very good in the wet and semi-wet and also had very good steering inputs.'

And of the comparison with Lando? 'Jenson was a very similar driver to Lando, I think,' Peter continued. 'I'm not sure Lando is as good as Jenson was, in terms of throttle application, power application. Jenson was so good in that area. I think it's difficult for anybody, apart from Perez, really to put their hand up and say that. But I think, in other ways, he was quite similar to Lando, the way Lando drives, and very, very rarely did you see Jenson with any sort of spike in his inputs or with a car appreciably out of line, just really good.

'Just great feel, fingertip touch in the wet because he was so supple and soft in the way he drove and the right foot and the brilliant foot coordination he had, still has probably!'

Off track, Button became a passionate triathlete, competing in events like the London Triathlon and IRONMAN 70.3 Santa Rosa, where he won his age group. He once said, 'It's great to show that we do have to train hard to be an F1 driver . . . we aren't just at home sitting around,' highlighting how seriously he took physical conditioning.

Jenson's career after 2009 brought further wins with McLaren, including memorable victories in changeable weather. His drive from last to first at the 2011 Canadian Grand Prix, which took over four hours in wet-dry conditions, is widely considered one of the greatest in modern F1. Button started seventh, collided with teammate Lewis Hamilton, received a drive-through penalty, dropped to 21st and last place, and still managed to win the race, overtaking Sebastian Vettel on the final lap. Button told the press afterwards, 'Everything went wrong up until I won the race.'

Jenson retired from full-time Formula 1 racing at the end of 2016, making a one-off return at the 2017 Monaco GP to replace Fernando Alonso. He ended his F1 career with a record of 15 Grand Prix wins, 50 podiums, one World Championship (2009), 306 race starts and a legacy as one of Formula 1's most versatile and admired champions.

Finally, as we complete this chapter on British greats from former eras, a round-up of two other drivers, plus some interesting facts about Brits on the track.

Let's begin with John Surtees, who won the F1 World Championship in 1964, driving for Ferrari. He claimed his first Grand Prix victory in his 27th race, showing he had made a steady rise through the ranks of F1. Surtees had already conquered the world of motorbikes, winning seven World Championships between 1956 and 1960. To this day, he remains the only man ever to win world titles in both motorbike Grands Prix and F1.

His transition from bikes to cars was brilliant, and his technical understanding of machinery made him unique in both. In recognition of his achievements, Surtees was inducted into the International Motorsports Hall of Fame in 1996. In 2003, the Federation of International Motorcycling honoured him as a Grand Prix Legend. His legacy continues to inspire racers who dream of mastering different forms of motorsport.

Johnny Herbert, renowned for his own brand of resilience and determination, won his first Formula 1 Grand Prix at Silverstone in 1995, a moment that delighted British fans. It was a long-awaited victory, coming at his 71st attempt, after years of battling injuries and inconsistent machinery. Championship contenders Michael Schumacher and Damon Hill collided, creating an opportunity for Herbert to take the lead and ultimately the win. The victory was particularly special as it occurred on home soil, in front of his home crowd.

Jenson Button had an even longer wait, achieving his maiden win at the Hungarian Grand Prix in August 2006, on his 113th attempt. That race, held in wet-dry conditions, showcased Button's smooth driving style and tactical brilliance. Eddie Irvine, who often played a supporting role to Michael Schumacher at Ferrari, finally broke through with a win at the 82nd attempt, at the 1999 Austrian GP, marking a key milestone in his career. These three drivers exemplify the perseverance required in Formula 1, where talent alone isn't always enough – engineering, timing, team dynamics and raceday execution all play a role.

Last, but far from least, let's hear it for Mike Hawthorn, who captured the imagination of the British public by becoming the first Briton ever to win the F1 World Championship. It was a landmark achievement that helped elevate the sport's popularity in the UK. He began racing in 1950 and made his Grand Prix debut in 1952.

While Lewis Hamilton would go on to win his first Grand Prix in just his sixth race, Hawthorn achieved his maiden victory in his ninth, driving for Ferrari at the French Grand Prix in 1953. Over the course of his career, he won three races from 45 starts, secured four pole positions and recorded six fastest laps. In 1958, he clinched the world title in the iconic Ferrari 246 Dino, narrowly beating Stirling Moss. Sadly, Hawthorn's life was cut short when he died in a road accident near Guildford, Surrey, on 22 January 1959, just three days before his 30th birthday. His legacy lives on as a pioneer of British motorsport – and the nation's first F1 world champion.

The Hawthorn Memorial Trophy was established in his honour and is awarded annually to the most successful British or Commonwealth F1 driver.

Mike's legacy is woven into the very fabric of British motorsport. He opened the door for the likes of Graham Hill, Jackie Stewart, Nigel Mansell and Lewis Hamilton – and he did it with such style, courage and determination to be a winner.

CHAPTER 4

FORMULA WON

In the last few weeks of autumn 2001, a 16-year-old lad from unfashionable Stevenage got his first taste of real car racing. Lewis Hamilton had already been a kart whizz around Britain and Europe, but now he stepped into a Formula Renault – a car that was heavier, louder and faster than the little karts in which he'd built his early name. The jump wasn't just about bigger machines; it meant more technical stress, more stamina, more thinking. It was in this challenging arena that his raw, outstanding talent and potential earned him what would be the most fateful meeting of his life.

Hamilton's debut in the Renault Winter Series was a clear 'I'm here' moment. He raced against men who'd been doing this for years and still managed a solid fifth place overall. That result caught the eye of Ron Dennis, the boss at McLaren. Dennis had watched Hamilton's karting run for a while and saw the obvious potential the boy possessed for a future Formula 1 champion. Their 'famous chat' from the karting days grew into a professional partnership, with Dennis providing the money and logistics that would lift Hamilton up the ladder to eventual legend.

Nothing was left to chance; each step of the ladder was designed to shape a future F1 driver. The move from karting to Formula Renault, then to Formula 3, followed a clear plan.

In 2002, Hamilton entered the British Formula Renault Championship. The calendar was longer, the opponents tougher. He shrugged it off, ending the season third overall with three wins, three fastest laps and three poles. Those numbers showed he could learn fast. At the same time, he raced four of the nine rounds of the Eurocup, earning one win, three more podiums and a fifth place in that series. This suggested he 'didn't need years to learn his trade' and that his 'apprenticeship' was pretty much over after a single senior season.

The next year felt almost historic. In 2003, Hamilton took the British Formula Renault title with ten wins, 11 poles and 419 points, clinching the championship two races before the end. His nearest rival, Alex Lloyd, only managed two victories and 377 points – a big gap that showed the mental edge Hamilton had built over the field. The dominance was not just raw speed; it was also a deep grasp of race strategy, car setup and how to squeeze performance from a machine.

At the tail end of 2003 he dipped his toe into British

Formula 3, running the last two rounds. It was 'just a taste' of the higher class, but it signalled the next step was inevitable and it was a preview of the hurdles awaiting in the higher tiers of motor racing.

Another key character in Lewis's inexorable rise was John Booth, head of Manor Motorsport. Booth helped move Hamilton from karting into cars and later recalled: 'McLaren asked us to give him a go . . . He was 16 and had never driven a car before. After a couple laps he went off. It wasn't a shock, but even then you could see he had something rare.' Booth's words summed up the boy: a rookie rawness mixed with a 'relentless hunger to improve' that pushed him past the usual mistakes a beginner made. With Booth's guidance and Manor's resources, Hamilton's natural speed turned into consistent, championship-winning performance.

At the same time, Lewis – under the strict instructions from dad Anthony – was living a kind of double life. Evenings he spent in garages, hunched over telemetry with engineers, while his friends were out at parties or playing video games. But he still managed to finish his GCSEs at John Henry Newman School in Stevenage and then signed up at the Cambridge College of Arts and Sciences – a small college that gave him a flexible timetable to fit his racing diary. A 2002 school newsletter summed up his situation: 'Lewis finds it hard to focus on school when his mind is on the weekend's race. Still, his grades are good. He now races in Formula Renault and hopes one day to reach Formula 1.' The quote shows the clash between the distraction of big dreams and his ability to keep his school work afloat, hinting at an intelligence to still do well in exams, and yet an ambition to be a champion beyond just junior racing.

All told, Hamilton's rise from a karting prodigy to a dominant force in junior formulae between 2001 and 2003 was no lucky stumble. It was a planned path, fuelled by huge talent, and propped up by a group of top mentors and a school that was willing to accommodate his schedule – in other words, to back him. Every decision seemed laid out on a map, every race a step towards a larger goal, and the support from people like his wily dad Anthony, Ron Dennis, John Booth and the Manor team turned raw speed into a future F1 hopeful. This all points to a bigger observation about motorsport talent: when vision, capability and the right institutional backing line up, a gifted youngster can become a champion.

By then, Hamilton also had another rite of passage to complete: learning to drive on ordinary roads. At 17, like countless other British teenagers, he began taking lessons. Unlike most, he passed his test after just six hours of instruction. His driving instructor, Stephen Sivell, knew immediately he was teaching someone unusual. 'He was quick – too quick,' Sivell said. 'I had to remind him this wasn't a racetrack. Corners aren't meant to be taken flat-out in a Micra!'

Hamilton had turned up to his first lesson dressed in white, wearing Oakley sunglasses. 'I thought, here we go, a boy racer,' Sivell remembered with amusement. But what really stood out was Hamilton's karting instinct. He took corners like a racer – swinging wide, cutting to the apex.

'That's not what examiners look for,' Sivell reminded him. Hamilton grinned, mischievous, as if enjoying the discomfort of his instructor.

Back on the track, the 2002 Formula Renault season began with high expectations. Hamilton had been fastest in testing, but fate intervened. He was taken out by a backmarker in the first race and went three rounds without a win. Doubts began to creep in. Then came Silverstone. Hamilton, running fifth on slick tyres as the rain began to fall, carved through the field with astonishing speed. He won comfortably. Booth later said: 'That was the turning point. His confidence soared. From then on, he was nearly untouchable.'

Still, the next rung on the ladder wasn't without difficulty. In his first Formula 3 appearance at Brands Hatch, Hamilton's debut ended in disaster. A puncture ended race one, while a collision with teammate Tor Graves in race two left Hamilton trapped in the car, complaining of back pain. Marshals carefully extracted him and he was taken to hospital for overnight observation. Motorsport.com drily commented that it was 'a debut he won't soon forget'.

But Hamilton was not the sort to be discouraged. In 2004, he joined Manor in the Formula 3 Euro Series. The results were modest by his standards, one victory, fifth overall, but he did take the Bahrain F3 Superprix. Booth later admitted the issue wasn't Hamilton but the machinery. 'Our car wasn't the best. And Lewis wants to win every-thing. It was tough, but he never lost his positivity. He just kept smiling.'

That smile was part of his armour. Ayrton Senna, the driver Hamilton was often compared to, had sometimes been cold and calculating in how he won people over. Hamilton didn't need to calculate; his warmth drew people in naturally.

By late 2004, the writing was on the wall, and it was super positive. McLaren arranged for him to test at Silverstone that December, and the following season they placed him with ASM, the powerhouse of Formula 3. The effect was immediate.

Hamilton's 2005 season was a rampage. He began with victory at Hockenheim and never looked back. By the end, he had 15 wins, 13 poles, ten fastest laps and the championship secured with four races still to run. For good measure, he also won the F3 Masters at Zandvoort, the Monaco F3 Grand Prix and the Pau Grand Prix. Formula 3's official site declared him the greatest driver in the series' history.

ASM boss Frédéric Vasseur – later to persuade Hamilton to join Ferrari and become his team boss there – admired not just the speed, but the attitude. 'If he had a bad qualifying, he didn't point fingers. He said, "That was my mistake. Don't touch the car." That honesty made him stand out.'

The next logical step was GP2, the final proving ground before Formula 1. In 2006, Hamilton joined ASM's sister team, ART Grand Prix. He adapted instantly, winning five races, including stunning double victories at both the Nürburgring and Silverstone. His charge at Silverstone, where he passed Nelson Piquet Jr and Clivio Piccione in a breathtaking move, was replayed around the world.

By the time he clinched the GP2 championship at Monza, the outcome was inevitable. Ron Dennis could not hold him back any longer.

In September 2006, Dennis invited Hamilton to his home. Over dinner, he delivered the words Hamilton had dreamed of hearing for nearly a decade: 'We've decided you'll be our driver next year.'

Hamilton later confessed that he tried to stay calm, offering only a small smile. But inside, he was overwhelmed.

The boy from Stevenage, who once told Ron Dennis he wanted to drive for McLaren, was about to see that dream made real. After nine years of preparation, sacrifice and brilliance, Lewis Hamilton was ready to step into Formula 1.

George Russell's progress through the junior categories of motor racing was more methodical but still shot through with excellence. His first season in single-seaters immediately marked him out as a driver with unusual composure. Russell quickly demonstrated his potential by entering the 2014 BRDC Formula 4 Championship in Britain. Driving for Lanan Racing, he adapted impressively to the demands of single-seater competition, showcasing both speed and consistency throughout the season.

His campaign culminated in a dramatic final race at Snetterton, where he secured the championship title by a narrow margin of three points over teammate Arjun Maini. This victory not only affirmed Russell's talent but also served as a springboard for his ascent through the junior motorsport ranks. As part of his prize, he earned a GP3 test with Arden Motorsport at the Yas Marina Circuit and received a £25,000 cash award – further opening doors to higher levels of competition. The BRDC Formula 4 title marked a pivotal moment in Russell's career, laying the foundation for his journey towards Formula 1.

The logical next step was European competition, and Formula Renault became his new proving ground. His time in the category exposed him to a higher calibre of rivals and a wider variety of circuits, from the grand venues of Europe to the gritty, lesser-known tracks that test drivers in ways no simulator can replicate. Russell was not always the quickest in raw speed, but his tenacity, overtaking craft and refusal to concede marked him as a racer of real substance. He took a notable victory in Spain and added several podiums, showing that even in fields dominated by more established names, he could carve out a presence. These performances led him naturally towards the FIA Formula 3 European Championship, where his next challenge awaited.

The switch to Formula 3 was a leap, but it was also where Russell began to refine the balance between aggression and control that would later become his hallmark. Driving first for Carlin, he endured an education in how relentlessly competitive the series could be. The margins were minuscule and the grids stacked with future Formula 1 talent, yet Russell quietly went about accumulating results. He earned wins, podiums and, more importantly, the kind of reputation that teams in the higher categories never overlook. His name circulated not simply as a driver with speed, but as someone with the tactical acumen to survive and thrive in unforgiving company.

When he moved to Hitech in his second year of European Formula 3, he was no longer only participating. He was contesting at the front, duelling with names like Lance Stroll and Maximilian Günther, and proving himself a perennial podium threat. He did not win the championship, but it was obvious that he took another step forward from the previous season.

Each season had offered tangible proof that his trajectory pointed in only one direction.

His performance with Hitech, a team powered by Mercedes engines, caught the attention of the Mercedes F1 team. By January 2017, Russell was officially signed to the Mercedes-AMG Petronas Formula 1 Team's junior programme, joining the ranks of Pascal Wehrlein and Esteban Ocon.

In 2017, Russell found the perfect platform in GP3 with the ART Grand Prix team. The outfit had a history of nurturing champions, and with Russell, they had someone who embraced the responsibility. Russell was known for his intense preparation – he studied data obsessively and worked closely with engineers to fine-tune performance. Even when technical issues struck (like at the Hungaroring), he managed to claw back positions and minimise damage. And rather than relying on dramatic overtakes or risky manoeuvres, he built his campaign on clean starts, race management and tyre strategy.

It wasn't about dazzling the crowd – it was about proving,

week after week, that he was the most complete driver on the grid. That kind of maturity at such a young age is what made Mercedes take him seriously.

Every weekend seemed to reaffirm his status as one of the brightest talents on the ladder. He started the season combining qualifying speed with Sunday execution, and the results flowed. He swept to the title not through moments of brilliance, but via an unbeatable combination of consistency and pace.

In 2018, Formula 2 called, and with ART, he again saw before him the greatest challenge one could imagine before Formula 1. But Russell treated F2 as if it was no problem and in the most impressive way possible – he won races from the start.

Winning twice at Silverstone, in front of his home crowd, felt like a coronation. He battled rivals such as Lando Norris and Alexander Albon throughout the year, but it was Russell's consistency, race management and calm under pressure that set him apart. He claimed the championship at the first attempt, earning his place as Britain's next Formula 1 prospect. George had clinched the title with 287 points, finishing 68 ahead of Lando.

But it wasn't only the trophies that made Russell's rise inevitable; it was also the way in which he attained them. He achieved them by combining clarity of thought with a strong belief in himself. Where others seemed to lack one or the other, Russell seemed to lack neither. When he was composing himself to drive, he always appeared completely at ease. In every way possible, he gave off the impression of being 'ready'. In fact, when Williams came calling in 2019, it wasn't so much a surprise development as a logical step in what had been an upward path seemingly visible to all since the moment he'd first started driving single-seaters.

While Russell is defined by the steadiness of his ascent, Lando Norris's is of the opposite trajectory, heading to the same destination but with irrepressible flair. When Norris first transitioned to driving cars, it seemed such a natural step that nobody could have imagined it being anything other than a smooth and fairly straightforward progression. He drove almost as if the cars were an extension of the karts he once dominated; his immediate adaptation to life in the Ginetta Junior Championship being proof of that. He wasn't simply learning his way around a racetrack; he was winning, and doing so with a mix of flamboyance and precision that had already made him a crowd favourite by the time the first season ended.

His next step was into the newly created British Formula 4 Championship in 2015. With Carlin, Norris transformed into a front-running force almost immediately. Over the course of the year he claimed eight victories, ten pole positions and the overall title.

This was a statement that he was capable of mastering any environment. The inevitable attention and acclaim he received at that stage of his career could have been a distraction, but Norris wore it lightly, his natural charm disarming and his focus remaining firmly on the track.

By 2016, his horizons stretched far wider than Britain. Norris ventured to New Zealand for the Toyota Racing

Series, a baptism in international racing against older, seasoned rivals. He didn't merely compete, though; he won the championship and the prestigious New Zealand Grand Prix, underlining once again his adaptability to different surroundings and challenges.

Returning to Europe, he launched into Formula Renault with extraordinary dominance, sweeping both the Eurocup and the Northern European Cup. Across both series he racked up a string of wins and poles. The talent was undeniable, and the momentum irresistible. He even found time to dip into British Formula 3, where he added yet more wins to his burgeoning résumé.

By year's end, Norris was a champion multiple times over, and the recipient of the McLaren Autosport BRDC Award, a prize that had propelled names like Button, Hamilton and Coulthard before him.

The following year he moved into European Formula 3 with Carlin, and it was here that Norris proved himself not just as a quick driver, but a complete one. The grid he faced was stacked with future Formula 1 talent, including George Russell and Mick Schumacher, but Norris clinched the title with two races to go. His season was built on nine wins, but also on relentless podium finishes that spoke of consistency and composure.

He shone at marquee events too, finishing second at the Macau Grand Prix, a race renowned as the ultimate test of nerve and skill in junior single-seaters. It was the kind of performance that etched his name firmly on the list of future stars.

The next natural progression was Formula 2, and in 2018 Norris entered the championship with Carlin. His season began with a flourish – victory in the opening race in Bahrain set the tone – but it was also a year of growing pains. Norris gathered podiums with regularity, yet he also experienced the harsh lessons of tyre degradation and the brutal competitiveness of F2. His rival George Russell often seemed one step ahead, but Norris nevertheless drove with distinction, finishing the year as runner-up. That he was not champion did little to dent his reputation; if anything, the duels with Russell sharpened both men, preparing them for what was to come.

Throughout his climb, Norris balanced the demands of racing with the expectations of representing McLaren, who had taken him under their wing. While climbing the F2 ladder, Norris was already leaning towards Formula 1. McLaren pushed him into FP1 sessions at Spa and Monza and he was given a role in testing programmes, including tyre development runs.

His youthful exuberance and media-friendly personality made him a natural fit for the modern era of the sport, but it was his underlying racecraft that ensured he would not be dismissed as mere hype.

By the time McLaren announced him as a full-time driver for 2019, there was no sense of surprise. Norris had been on a fast track from the moment he left junior karting behind. Each championship, each season, had been a step forward, proof of an innate ability to adapt and excel.

Where Russell's rise had the feel of an inexorable march,

Norris's was more like a whirlwind – fast, colourful and impossible to ignore.

Both men mastered Formula 3 and Formula 2, and both demonstrated qualities that made Formula 1 inevitable. Russell carried the calculation and sheer determination of a driver destined to endure. Norris brought the sparkle and instinct of a driver destined to excite. In their own ways, both were ready when Formula 1 came calling.

The careers of Hamilton, Russell and Norris in the years between Formula 3 and Formula 2 reveal not just three individual stories, but a study in how talent, opportunity and character play a key role on the road to the land of milk and honey that is F1. Each man arrived in F3 and F2 with a reputation already established, but how they performed when the lights went out made their subsequent rise to F1 a formality.

Hamilton's maiden year in the Euro Series with Manor produced flashes of brilliance but only modest results. It was a reminder that even the most naturally gifted can be held back by cars not quite equal to their ambition.

Yet that season proved valuable not for what it lacked, but for what it revealed: a refusal to be floored by setbacks, an ability to keep his head high and his motivation intact even when victories seemed distant.

The following season with ASM showed the true Hamilton unleashed. With competitive equipment beneath him, he dominated the field, racking up wins with fearless overtaking that marked him out as exceptional.

It was not simply that he won races; it was the manner

in which he did so, battling through to the front of the pack like a veteran.

By the time he stepped into GP2, the championship felt like a formality. That he won it at his first attempt only confirmed what his Formula 3 season had already suggested – here was a driver who would rise to every level given the opportunity.

Russell's journey, by contrast, was marked more by steady success. His European Formula 3 seasons were hard-fought, and littered with moments of both triumph and frustration. He was never the overwhelming force that Hamilton had been, nor did he sweep the board in the way Norris would. Instead, his rise was one of gradual sharpening, intelligent racecraft and a steady temperament.

In his time with Carlin and later Hitech, he grew into a driver who could think ahead. It paid dividends when he arrived in GP3 with ART. There, he was not the most flamboyant driver on the grid, but he was one of the most complete. He qualified strongly, managed races cleverly and looked like a driver who expected to succeed.

His Formula 2 campaign was similarly consistent, controlled and ended with him as a champ. Hamilton had blazed a trail, but Russell built his success race by race.

Norris brought yet another dimension to their differing roads to the top. If Hamilton embodied inevitability and Russell calculation, Norris represented pure flair. His Formula 3 season with Carlin was a statement of determined intent. He was a natural and seemed to thrive easily as the laps sped by. Nine wins and a host of podiums sealed the championship, and he did it in style.

Even in Macau, where he missed out on victory, his performance had the fans acclaiming his raw talent. His rookie year began with a win in Bahrain that suggested another runaway campaign, but the season quickly settled into a grind. Tyre management, strategy calls and the relentlessness of the competition tested him in new ways, and in Russell he found a rival who seemed to have mastered those elements more completely.

Norris finished runner-up, an impressive achievement, but the contrast with Russell was telling: where George looked like the finished article, Lando still looked like a work in progress.

To compare the trio directly, Hamilton stood apart for the sheer decisiveness with which he dismantled each category. His Formula 3 and GP2 titles were part of a process that saw him move forward relentlessly. Russell's rise lacked that sparkle, but in its place came a reliability that teams value as highly as raw speed – he could be trusted to deliver.

Norris's trajectory was perhaps the most human. He may not have carried the crushing inevitability of Hamilton or the cold calculation of Russell, but his capacity to delight with a daring move gave him a quality all his own.

Threaded through both Russell's and Norris's stories is Hamilton's shadow. By the time they were contesting Formula 3 and Formula 2, Hamilton was already a global icon, his achievements having redefined what was possible for a young British driver on the international stage. For Russell, Hamilton was both inspiration and benchmark. He has admitted as much, describing Hamilton as 'the greatest driver of all time' and 'the type of person that every racing driver should aspire to be'.

To see Hamilton succeed so completely was to know that British talent, given the right circumstances, could thrive against the world's best. It was so inspirational and motivational for Norris, and Russell.

Hamilton provided a foundation and was a beacon. His success ensured that programmes and teams were more willing to invest in British juniors, knowing that the pay-off could be immense. His example lit the way, setting a standard they knew would be difficult to achieve, but at least they had a yardstick with which to work. For Russell and Norris, Hamilton wasn't just a hero – he was the reason the system believed in them.

Their individual stories highlight three different ways to reach the very top. Hamilton's brilliance was immediate, Russell's measured, Norris's mercurial. Each found success in their own way, each wrestled with their own failings, but all three proved that the junior formulas are worthwhile grounding fields, shaping talents who would go on to carry the hopes of their own generation. Hamilton led the way, Norris and Russell followed him, learned from him and benefited from his direction.

CHAPTER 5

DEBUT DAZE

The Australian city of Melbourne has played a massive part in the lives of Hamilton, Norris and Russell. It is where they all made their Formula 1 debuts – Lewis in 2007 and the other duo in 2019. The Albert Park track has known its share of controversies and dramas since it was chosen as the new regular season opener in 1996, taking the role from Adelaide, which hosted the event for a decade from 1985 to 1995. Only Bahrain has also played host for the opening round in 2006, 2010, 2021 and 2022.

Albert Park is loved by fans for its much-improved facilities and stands when compared with Adelaide. They also like that it's a semi-street circuit, using the roads that run around Albert Park Lake. For 11 months of the year, these are open to normal traffic – cars, buses, cyclists, joggers and dog walkers all share them. Some parts of the circuit – like the pit straight and paddock – are constructed specially for

Formula 1 and aren't used by everyday traffic. And barriers, grandstands and run-off areas are all brought in and removed for the race weekend, like a traditional street circuit.

Fans say it adds to the feel of being at a street race, like Monaco, and they can get closer to the action.

Drivers have a more mixed view of the place while admitting it is unique with its street circuit merged with parkland track set-up. Jenson Button, for instance, enjoyed the challenge of racing there, saying, 'Albert Park is a tricky place to start the season . . . an unforgiving, technical, bumpy street circuit, but that's why we love driving there.' And Lance Stroll is another fan: 'The circuit has a nice flow and is fast-paced.' However, as with Monaco, there are few opportunities to overtake and David Coulthard once admitted it was far from being the most challenging of circuits.

Technically, there is much for debut drivers to cope with. Braking demands are moderate – not as hard on the brakes as circuits like Montreal or Monza. Grip is initially a problem as the public roads are used most of the year. Overtaking, as Coulthard once said, is tricky – like Monaco – although layout changes in 2021 and multiple DRS zones have improved opportunities to do so. Teams usually run a medium-downforce package to balance speed on straights with grip in the fast corners.

The track itself has presented varying challenges at varying stages of development over the years – primarily to prove wrong the doubters who had criticised it as a non-overtaking friendly set-up.

Here's a list of some of the improvements – Turn 1 and 2 (Brabham Straight into Jones): A high-speed braking zone after the start/finish straight, a prime overtaking spot. The layout was widened in 2022 to allow multiple racing lines, enhancing overtaking chances. Turns 3 and 4: Tight right-left combination, often a hotspot for first-lap incidents. High-speed potential (Turns 9–11): Revised in 2021 to remove a slow chicane, making this section much quicker and creating a new DRS zone. Final sector: The modern layout now has 14 corners, where it once had 16. It includes Turns 13 and 14, which are challenging. Turn 13 was widened to improve cornering speed, and Turn 14 leads directly on to the pit straight, providing braking and traction risks for the drivers.

But challenges such as Turns 13 and 14 were what our British debutant trio had been primed for. This was where the training scheme at McLaren, especially in the simulator, that Hamilton and Norris had benefited from – and Russell's Mercedes teachings – played a huge role. They may have been novices in Melbourne but they certainly weren't without engineering and driving know-how.

Yet it is correct to say they were Albert Park virgins because they had never raced there – as the venue is used purely for Formula 1 and the local regional support races that travel with it. The traditional support bill in Melbourne has been: Formula Ford Australia, V8 Supercars/Supercars Championship, Porsche Carrera Cup and other regional or promotional series. Crucially, F2 and F3 have never raced at Albert Park. They have never shipped out to Australia because of costs and logistics (flying whole grids and support crews halfway around the world for one race simply isn't feasible for the lower Formula races).

It all meant that if you were an Aussie who had come up through the ranks, you had an advantage even before debuting at Albert Park in F1 as you knew the track. You'd already raced there. Our Brit trio's first experience of it would be in practice after they arrived on the Thursdays in March 2007 and 2019, but they soon settled into the groove at the track.

Drivers often say another positive feature of Albert Park on a Formula 1 weekend is its intimacy; they tend to sit out and chat with each other behind the garages. Maybe because it's the traditional curtain-raiser there is a friendliness and empathy between the teams that certainly evaporates by the time Formula 1 hits Europe months later.

By then, intense rivalries have been established and the whole business is much more cut-throat. Lewis Hamilton didn't feel under pressure as he prepared for his race back in 2007. He relaxed with his father Anthony, having a chat and a glass of lemonade in a deckchair in between practice and qualifying.

Why should he feel anxious? It was what he'd worked his whole life towards. His F1 debut, all those days of struggle and hardship with his dad, the highs and lows, the commitments, everything that he'd put in over his 'lost' childhood. Now was the moment to show the world who he was and what he could do.

Ironically, all the limelight, all the attention, was still on his McLaren team, but not on him. His co-driver Fernando

Alonso, the double world champion, was also making his debut for his new team. This was the man who had won at Melbourne the previous season and who was expected to win again, this time for a new team at the start of the 2007 campaign. It was certainly an unusual scenario: two men making their debut in the same team at the same time.

One driver was a rookie competing in his first F1 race ever. The other was a two-time reigning world champion switching teams (from Renault). Both started their 'eras' at McLaren in the same weekend.

The press were inquisitive about the boy racer who would drive alongside the world champion. Team boss Ron Dennis had been largely successful in keeping Lewis out of their grasp for many years, but now allowed his protégé to answer some questions at a pre-race conference. Asked what the key to his arrival in F1 had been, and what his hopes were for the race, Lewis replied simply and honestly.

He said, 'I am motivated by a desire to be the best at whatever I decide to put my mind to. Once I have decided to take up a challenge, my inner self will not let me give up unless I have achieved my goal. I love motor racing and I have done so since I first watched it on TV when I was about five. The key element in all of this is that I am not here to take part, I am here to win, and I will do whatever mentally and physically it takes to achieve that in due course. I do not plan to waste this opportunity.'

He showed maturity when asked about how he thought he and Alonso would get on. With comments that would hardly represent the rancour that would develop between the pair as the season progressed, he answered, 'It is truly an honour for me to be given this opportunity to work alongside Fernando in my first year as a Formula 1 driver. I have a tremendous amount of respect for what he has achieved.

'The sheer size of the challenge of working with him and competing against him is what is most exciting. All of my former teammates have been hugely competitive and the challenge and excitement comes from having to find the answers to the most important question, "Just how far do I need to push myself to beat that person and just how far can I go?"

'With Fernando being a two-time world champion, I know I have to dig deeper than ever before, which is what I love about being a racing driver.' It was his dream come true to make his debut for McLaren, 'The feeling is indescribable. Growing up, I always dreamed of racing for McLaren and now I am. The thought of racing and working with my teammates is a great feeling; to be driving a Vodafone McLaren Mercedes is literally surreal.'

When teams hire a rookie, they often pair them with an established teammate to provide stability and mentorship – though there are exceptions, such as Max Verstappen and Carlos Sainz both debuting as rookies at Toro Rosso in 2015. Conversely, when a world champion joins a new team, they're usually paired with an experienced driver, as seen when Sebastian Vettel joined Ferrari in 2015 alongside Kimi Räikkönen.

Hamilton didn't look at all out of place, rookie or not, as he took to the track in Melbourne in 2007. In the first practice session, he posted the fourth-fastest time, just 1.664 seconds behind session leader Fernando Alonso.

For George Russell, in 2019, it was a much more testing first practice at Albert Park. The Williams FW42 was significantly off the pace. Russell and teammate Robert Kubica ended up 19th and 20th, nearly four seconds slower than the leaders.

Norris completed 22 laps in FP1. His best lap time was 1:24.669, placing him 18th overall in the session. He was well off Lewis Hamilton's fastest FP1 time of 1:23.599. Norris's real statement of intent came in qualifying, where he outpaced both Alfa Romeos, Racing Points and even his teammate, Carlos Sainz.

In 2007, Hamilton posted the fourth-fastest lap in final qualifying, timed at 1:26.755. It placed him just behind teammate Alonso (P2) and BMW's Nick Heidfeld (P3), with Kimi Räikkönen taking pole. A brilliant few days' practice and qualifying highlighted that he definitely hadn't come to make up the numbers: he was in Melbourne to win, or at least to finish on the podium.

In 2019, Norris also showed he wasn't in Albert Park as an overawed newcomer. He reached Q3, outperforming expectations and becoming the fastest Renault-powered car on the grid. His lap time in Q3 was 1:22.304, a standout result for a rookie and McLaren's best qualifying performance in years. It left him in eighth position on the grid, on the fourth row, for the race.

Meanwhile, Russell was eliminated in Q1, driving the struggling FW42, which was significantly off the pace.

His best lap was 1:24.360, nearly two seconds slower than the Q2 cut-off. Norris's debut was widely praised, while Russell's was more overlooked due to the limitations of his car. Yet Russell, who started 19th, had outpaced teammate Kubica, giving an indication of what he could do if he had the right machinery. The problem wasn't with him; it was with the car.

As the lights went out in Melbourne in 2019, Norris opened the throttle and looked determined to move up the field swiftly. But Albert Park's opening corners are tight, and for a rookie, that can spell trouble amid the mayhem of a race. Caught in the midfield chaos, Norris lost ground early and settled into twelfth.

The real frustration began around lap ten. He found himself stuck behind Antonio Giovinazzi, whose Alfa Romeo was limping through a long opening stint on worn tyres. Norris clearly had more pace but couldn't get past him. Lap after lap, he appeared glued to Giovinazzi's rear wing, watching the gap to the cars ahead stretch out.

McLaren made a strategic move, calling Norris in early to try an undercut. But even after the stop, he rejoined into more traffic, still boxed in and unable to unleash his speed. After the race, Norris didn't attempt to sugarcoat it: 'I made a couple of mistakes that put me outside of it . . . I feel I let McLaren down a bit.' It was a tough self-assessment, but typical of the world-class driver he was to become.

George Russell's first taste of Formula 1 also came with a bit of a reality check. Starting from 19th on the grid in a Williams that was well off the pace, his debut was less about racing and more about enduring. As the race got under way, Russell kept his nose clean through the opening corners, avoiding any coming together. But with the FW42 lacking grip, downforce and straight-line speed, he was quickly isolated at the back of the field. There wasn't much chance to show that here was a potential world champ in waiting. Just a lonely drive, two seconds off the midfield and falling further behind with each lap.

Still, Russell did what he could. He kept the car on track, managed his tyres and executed a clean race without mistakes. It wasn't glamorous, but in a car that was nearly undriveable, it was an impressive show of professionalism. He finished 16th, two laps down, but ahead of teammate Kubica, who had a more troubled run. There were no overtakes for a future highlights reel, but there was composure.

As Russell said afterwards, he had done his absolute best and would keep plugging away in the Williams. He was a tad despondent but hadn't lost any self-confidence or belief: like everyone else, he knew the car was more or less a dud. He told reporters, 'I feel happy that I brought the car home with no dramas. It was a good first race from my side but obviously it is disappointing that we are so far behind the pace.'

Both he and Norris had handled the challenges of a debut F1 Grand Prix in their own typical styles. Norris showed his natural flair in qualifying, then the self-critical streak afterwards that he has often displayed in more recent F1 travails. Russell showed calmness in the face of a dismal car, making the best of what he had. Neither debut was headline-grabbing in terms of podiums or points, but both men emerged with credit. Norris proved he had raw speed to mix it with the best. Russell demonstrated that even towards the back of the pack, he possessed the discipline and calm mentality of a future F1 hero.

Norris had a car capable of Q3 heroics, but traffic and track position blunted his race. Russell had a car that condemned him to the rear, but made up for it with his strength of character. For Norris, twelfth place was the beginning of a journey that would soon see him on podiums. For Russell, 16th was a lesson in patience and perseverance that eventually carried him into a Mercedes seat.

Twelve years earlier, there had been no sign of consolation or commiserations as Hamilton roared home on his debut in the McLaren. It was a totally different scenario after a race in which he had finished on the podium – third, in his first F1 outing. A remarkable outcome. This would be the sort of statement that Norris and Russell would use as a yardstick for their own hopes of future success; Hamilton had shown he had no time to lose – he wanted to hit the very top, and quickly. No more learning or waiting for when the time was ripe. For Hamilton, that time was right now.

He had said as much in that pre-race press conference interview: 'If you want to be the best at whatever career you choose in life, then you have to compete at the very top. Formula 1 is the pinnacle of motorsport. From the time I started my racing career in Cadet Karts in 1994, right the way through to Formula Renault, Formula 3 and GP2, I have dedicated my life to achieving my goal of becoming a Formula 1 world champion. I am now another huge step closer to reaching my ultimate dream.'

He also explained how the adrenaline rush of racing was like an addiction to him, and he wanted it more and more: 'The feeling you get when you are really driving on the edge and pushing beyond the limit. The rush you get, the feeling of speed, the force that your body is under, all of that coming together gives the biggest adrenaline buzz and it's something that you can't experience anywhere else.'

And who from the past had he looked up to on the track, and who would he love to emulate on it now? Inevitably, two of the greatest, most exciting drivers ever. 'I would say that I haven't really had a hero since I was very young as a hero is someone that seems invincible. There are people that I greatly admire, though. In Formula 1, Ayrton Senna was really inspirational to me and I didn't think Michael Schumacher would ever be counted as a hero, but I really do look up to him for what he has achieved and what he has done for the sport.'

Finally, he was on the Albert Park track. The talking was over, and it was time to walk the walk. But he didn't walk, he ran, such was his nerveless approach and ability to live with the best drivers of the day. Rookie in name, not in outcome. During the first and second sessions, he showed he already had a feel for the car and a speed to be right up there with world champion teammate Alonso.

Yet after those sessions, he still spoke like a rookie, his innocent enthusiasm apparent. He said: 'I was so excited when I drove out of the garage for the first time this morning;

it was an incredible feeling as I have wanted to be a Formula 1 driver since I started karting, and now I am and enjoying every single moment. The track is good, particularly as I love street circuits, and the whole atmosphere is amazing. Back at the McLaren Technology Centre we have done a lot of simulation work to prepare me for this weekend, but it was good to actually drive it for real. The car feels good and the two sessions today were really useful.'

In qualifying, the excellence would continue and Hamilton, on his debut, ended fourth on the grid on Sunday. Eventual race winner Kimi Räikkönen, in the Ferrari, took pole in a time of 1:26.072, Alonso was second in 1:26.493 and BMW's Nick Heidfeld third in 1:26.556. Lewis clocked 1:26.755. After qualifying, the rookie voice returned: 'I'm overwhelmed to be on the second row for my first Grand Prix – a huge thank you to the team who have worked so hard, both here at the track and back at base. This weekend is what I have been preparing myself for during the past 13 years and I'm enjoying every moment. I think we are in with a good chance in the race. Basically, I want to get a good start and then work hard to score as many points for the team and myself. I'm not going to make any predictions because anything can happen, but so far, so good.'

The race itself would see the same four who finished top in qualifying finish in the top four, but with Lewis and Heidfeld changing places. A crowd of 105,000 swarmed Albert Park for the first race of the 'post-Schumacher' era; the German's final race being the Brazilian Grand Prix on 22 October 2006.

Hamilton never looked out of place. Ice-cool, decisive and brilliant, he even matched the fierce pace of Räikkönen's Ferrari, while driving with a maturity beyond his years to keep Alonso at bay for the best part of the 58-lap race. He only fell behind the Spaniard when Alonso pulled off a short second pit stop to emerge ahead of him.

Hamilton's podium continued the glory run for British drivers at the circuit since its opening in 1996. Damon Hill won the inaugural event that year in the Williams and the following year, David Coulthard triumphed for McLaren. Eddie Irvine won in 1999 – his first Formula 1 win for Ferrari – and four years later, Coulthard notched up his second victory at Melbourne for McLaren.

Damon Hill, at that stage Britain's last F1 world champ, was on analysis duty for Hamilton's debut and said he was impressed by what he had witnessed. 'Lewis qualified well, and he raced brilliantly. He was at the sharp end in his first Grand Prix and was competitive with his teammate – really, really good.'

He admired how 'the weight of expectation was massive on Lewis and it seemed to me he didn't really show any sign of weakness at all. He was on it right from the word go. His start was just a classic, fantastic, pulling that move on the first corner. It was a brave, but committed, overtaking manoeuvre. It's very, very easy for someone in their first Grand Prix to make a hash of that, but he never looked like he was fazed by what he was doing – he just did it and it came off.

'And when he was in front of Fernando [Alonso], you

could see he was really using the entire road. He was right up against the wall going into the switchback at the back of Melbourne and he was using all the road on the exit. He was pushing, he was confident and he never looked ragged. It was good. He looked very happy on the podium. I think he knew he'd done a bloody good job. He was in the race at the sharp end in his first ever Grand Prix and competitive with his teammate. Tremendous – really, really good!'

Jenson Button had a disappointing weekend, finishing 15th, but also found time to congratulate Lewis. 'He did a fantastic job. Lewis had a great first race and was lucky enough to be in a good car, but there is no getting away from the fact that he did a great job.' Hamilton's third-place finish was the best debut result by a British racer in 41 years since Mike Parkes took second place in the French Grand Prix. Lewis finished 11.3 seconds behind Alonso who, in turn, was 7.2 seconds behind flying Finn Räikkönen. His result meant that he had also become the first Formula 1 rookie to claim a podium finish since Jacques Villeneuve in 1996.

After the event, Lewis was overjoyed, but also took time out at the post-race press conference to say he was indebted to his mechanics and technical support team: 'I'm absolutely ecstatic – today's result is more than I ever dreamed of achieving on my Grand Prix debut. A big thank you to the team who have worked so hard during the winter to make sure I was as prepared as I could possibly be. I made a good start, but the BMWs were quick off the line and Kubica managed to get past.

'There was no room on the inside so I got on the left and managed to outbrake both Kubica and Fernando coming into the first corner to take third. The race was intense and I was working very hard. I made a few mistakes, but nothing major and really enjoyed myself. It was great to lead the race for a few laps, but I knew it was only a temporary thing. 'Fernando got past me at the second pit stop as he was able to stay out a bit longer and I lost some time behind backmarkers.'

Meanwhile, phone-ins and website forums in the UK were buzzing. One fan called his performance remarkable, especially as it compared so favourably with teammate Fernando Alonso. 'This is the finest all-round driver in the world, a double world champion. Someone who last year took on and beat in a straight fight Michael Schumacher – who some consider to be the greatest ever and who was certainly the greatest of his generation.

'And yet Hamilton had the temerity to pass the illustrious Spaniard around the outside at the start and make him work hard for the rest of the race. You could count on one hand the number of drivers who could do that to Alonso in the same car, let alone on their Grand Prix debut. He made his mark in quite emphatic style and there is no doubt that Alonso, and the rest of the Formula 1 field, will have taken notice.'

There was a hell of a lot more comment and analysis on Hamilton's showing in 2007 than there was on Norris and Russell's in 2019. Inevitably perhaps, given that the latter duo didn't have the profile of Hamilton – his tough background and being the circuit's first black driver – and also that they didn't fare nearly as well in the race, Lando finishing 12th and George 19th. Neither were immediately viewed as sensations, as was Lewis, or potential world champions in waiting. Neither ripped up the form book or performed wildly beyond expectations.

It showed in F1 fans' reactions and comments on social media. It was more of a 'Well, they did OK, but let's wait and see' summary – as the following examples illustrate. On Reddit, one fan said, 'Norris got quite unlucky in this race, in my opinion. McLaren surely has a car capable of getting in the mix, and I expect them to be scoring very soon.

'Williams, on the other hand . . . I have a feeling that given the car's current state, it would be quite a miracle for either Russell or Kubica to score in the foreseeable future.' Another fan piped up, 'I think Norris did well in his first race.'

On the RaceFans site, several fans felt Lando showed great promise. One said, 'He has nothing to feel bad about . . . good to see him pushing himself.' Another added, 'It wasn't great but it certainly wasn't bad for a rookie.' While a third wrote, 'He did very well for his first race . . . made virtually no mistakes.'

On Reddit, fans had sympathy for Russell's plight in a difficult car. 'That Williams is just so bad. Even with Daniel's [Ricciardo] slow lap and pit stop after the first lap, he was catching Russell, who was on the medium by a second a lap while on the hard tyre. I'd be shocked if they ever made it out of the bottom two places on merit, let alone scoring points.'

Another commented, also sympathetically, pointing out that George had outperformed his much more experienced teammate Kubica: 'I spent FP2 at the fast Turn 11-12 complex, the Williams cars seemed planted through there, so I feel that the oversteering and drive control issues they had last year aren't their problem this year. Their turning seemed a bit slower than the rest, maybe it's just a slow car, maybe it's some understeer.

'Russell did alright, he kept up with a pack of cars. Kubica had a bit of a shocker. Sure, he broke his front wing, but after he pitted for a wing change and rejoined the track, in terms of track location he was quite far ahead of Russell, maybe 30 seconds or so. But Russell slowly whittled down that gap and lapped Kubica.'

It was the same on RaceFans, 'At least their new rookie George Russell seems to be doing all he can.'

Fans on other social media and mainstream sites agreed in principle that George had suffered a bad day at the office because of the car, and that if it continued he'd likely not be at Williams next season. That he deserved to be driving for a team that had a chance of performing well, and that he was a fine prospect – much like Lando, who had the benefit in their debut F1 season of being in the much-better car.

Neither shook F1 up as Lewis Hamilton had done on his debut – then again few on the circuit over the years have ever matched that exceptional performance.

CHAPTER 6

SILVER DREAM RACERS

It would be remiss to pen a book on the three current British F1 heroes — with appropriate nods to their gallant predecessors — and not devote a chapter to their exploits at the home of British racing cars, Silverstone. Both Hamilton and Norris have enjoyed recent successes at the Northamptonshire track, while Russell's day in the sun will surely follow, given the resources Mercedes are pumping into his future.

When Silverstone opened in 1948, it hardly looked like the fantastic home of British motor racing it now is. A disused RAF bomber station airfield in Northamptonshire, hastily transformed into a racing circuit, became the stage for the RAC International Grand Prix, widely regarded as the first British Grand Prix of the modern era.

Two years later, in May 1950, it hosted the first race of

the new Formula 1 World Championship. The race was won by Giuseppe 'Nino' Farina in an Alfa Romeo in front of the watching King George VI. The early years offered little British glory. The sport was dominated by continental giants like Alfa Romeo, Ferrari and Maserati.

Yet, Silverstone's very existence meant Britain now had a permanent home for racing. And British drivers quickly determined to make their mark at the venue.

The 1960s marked the first British success, thanks to Jim Clark. In 1963, Clark produced one of the most dominant performances seen on the circuit. Driving the Lotus 25, with its revolutionary monocoque chassis, he started from pole and never looked back, winning with ease. What made the day even more remarkable was the sight of fellow Brits John Surtees and Graham Hill completing the podium. Refuelling was allowed but the cars were all so close together that Clark couldn't sneak into the pits and had to run the last laps in all top gears to conserve his fuel.

It was an all-British top three, a declaration that the nation had finally arrived at the forefront of Formula 1.

Clark would go on to win at Silverstone again, in 1965 and 1967, becoming a symbol of British mastery. His calm precision and speed made him one of the sport's most admired characters. In '65, his engine was running out of oil so he had to coast through the corners. Graham Hill followed him home in second place. In '67, it looked as if the result would be reversed, with Hill the victor. But he unluckily suffered a rear suspension failure on lap 54 while leading, and Clark took advantage. It ended hopes of a Lotus 1-2 on home tarmac.

John Surtees, already a world champion biker, made history by becoming Formula 1 world champion in 1964 with Ferrari, the only person ever to achieve that feat on both two and four wheels. And Graham Hill's 1968 championship season, driving a Lotus-Ford, gave British fans another hero to cheer for – although, in an unlikely quirk, he never won the British Grand Prix. His son Damon did, in July 1994, in that fractious duel with disqualified Michael Schumacher, an incident we documented earlier in this book.

In 1969, Jackie Stewart added his name to the Brit parade of victors, winning in the Matra-Ford MS 80. He and Jochen Rindt had battled closely for supremacy throughout the race but Rindt was forced to make a pit stop and Jackie took full advantage.

Jackie also won in 1971, in a Tyrell Ford 003 – and went on to lift the World Drivers' Championship. And the much-loved fans' hero, James Hunt, roared to victory at Silverstone in 1977. He started on pole in the McLaren-Ford M26 but dropped to fourth after getting off to a disappointing start. But he then passed Jody Scheckter and outbraked Niki Lauda to finally take the lead, and the win, after John Watson retired.

New British heroes emerged. In 1981, Watson himself gave Britain one of its most unlikely victories. Driving for McLaren in the MP4, Watson was never considered the flashiest or the fastest of drivers. But he was admired for his intelligence and ability to outthink opponents.

At Silverstone, he delivered his only British Grand Prix win in the McLaren MP4/1, which was the first F1 car with a carbon fibre monocoque chassis. His victory came after Renault's René Arnoux and Alain Prost, who had dominated qualifying, faltered during the race. The home crowd roared in appreciation, not simply because he was British, but because Watson represented the honest, hard-working racer who always made the most of the talent he had. He was a supreme grafter and the fans admired him for always giving his all.

No discussion of British glory at Silverstone could ever leave out Nigel Mansell. If Clark embodied elegance and Stewart precision, Mansell was the showman – the fighter who seemed to carry the hopes of every British F1 fan on his shoulders.

His 1987 victory remains one of the most electrifying races the circuit has ever witnessed. Chasing down his Williams teammate Nelson Piquet, Mansell drove with fury. With just three laps to go, he launched a daring move at Stowe Corner, sweeping past Piquet to take the lead. The crowd erupted. His victory lap, running on fumes after his car had run low on fuel, only deepened the love affair between driver and fans.

Four years later, in 1991, he repeated the feat – this time famously giving Ayrton Senna a lift back to the pits after Senna's car failed. The image of Senna perched on the side of Mansell's car remains one of Formula 1's most iconic snapshots.

Nigel was once again on the podium as the winner in

1992. Again, he dominated the race, taking a lead of three seconds after the first lap! Damon Hill made his GP debut in this race, coming home in 16th.

Just two years later, Damon had progressed so fast in the sport that he ended up as a winner at Silverstone. He battled with Schumacher for much of the race and triumphed when the German received a ten-second penalty for a stop-go infringement. Princess Diana presented him with the winner's trophy. His win was emotional, coming two months after Ayrton Senna's death at Imola. Hill had been Senna's teammate at Williams, and after his death, he stepped into a leadership role for the rest of the season.

For British fans, watching another Hill once again stand atop the podium at their home race was a poignant moment in British motor racing: the passing of the torch from one generation to the next.

Johnny Herbert's victory in 1995 was a different kind of fairy tale. Once considered one of Britain's brightest prospects, Herbert's career had been nearly derailed by a horrific 1988 head-on smash into a wall in Formula 3000 at Brands Hatch. That he even made it to Formula 1 was remarkable; that he won the British Grand Prix a dream come true after the nightmare of his accident. Driving for Benetton, Herbert inherited the lead after a collision between Michael Schumacher and Damon Hill took both rivals out. Herbert held his nerve, and when he crossed the line to win, the Silverstone crowd erupted with admiration. It was more than just a race result – it was the culmination of years of perseverance, and the fans recognised it as such.

The final race of the decade saw a new Scots hero follow in the hallowed footsteps of Sir Jackie Stewart. David Coulthard's triumph in 1999 was special as it came in the era of Michael Schumacher's growing dominance.

Coulthard delivered under pressure to claim victory. It had looked as if Mika Häkkinen was on course for the victory but he had problems with a rear wheel and was forced off on lap 29. David kept his cool to bring the McLaren/Mercedes MP4/14 home in style.

Just as he had ended the '70s with that win for Britain, so Coulthard started the '80s with another. He won his second successive British GP at Silverstone, in the updated MP4/15, after overtaking Rubens Barrichello at Stowe on lap 31.

And then came Lewis Hamilton. The undisputed King of Silverstone, with nine victories from 2008 to 2024.

Then a slight change of the guard from the old era British hit parade to the new idols, with a 2025 win for Lando Norris.

Plus, George Russell wasn't doing too badly at the old track, either. A win for him at Silverstone would surely happen one day, the fans and the press agreed in 2025.

But Hamilton set the yardstick for all other pretenders to follow . . . whether fellow Brits or foreign drivers.

If Mansell stirred passions and Clark embodied grace, Hamilton brought a combination of talent, tenacity and charisma that made him the ultimate Silverstone hero. His first win in 2008 was nothing short of legendary. In torrential rain, Hamilton drove with astonishing control, lapping almost the entire field.

It was the kind of performance that comes only once in a generation, and it signalled that Hamilton was destined for greatness.

From there, he made Silverstone his fortress. Between 2014 and 2017, he won four British Grands Prix in a row, sending the home fans into wild celebrations each year. Each victory carried its own story: in 2019, a hard-fought duel with Mercedes teammate Valtteri Bottas; in 2020, a finish on three tyres after a last-lap puncture; in 2021, a controversial but decisive win after colliding with Max Verstappen; and in 2024, when many thought his best days were over, a return to the glory days win.

With nine British Grand Prix wins, Hamilton holds a record unlikely ever to be matched, his relationship with Silverstone etched into the history of the British racetrack. It's not for nothing that he has even had a section of the track named after him. In 2020, the British Racing Drivers' Club renamed the International Pits straight of the circuit as the Hamilton Straight – to honour Lewis for his record-breaking achievements, including his seventh Formula 1 World Championship and his numerous wins at Silverstone. The Hamilton Straight is unique as it is the only part of the track to be named after an individual driver.

At the time, Silverstone itself issued a statement to explain in more detail why they had decided on the honour: 'The owners of Silverstone, the British Racing Drivers' Club (BRDC), felt this unique honour was an appropriate way to recognise Lewis cementing his position as the most successful driver in the history of Formula 1, at the end of a remarkable season in which he equalled Michael Schumacher's seven World Championships and surpassed the German legend's total number of race wins.

'David Coulthard, President of the BRDC, broke the good news to Lewis, who has been a Member of the Club since 2006, this afternoon in Abu Dhabi. The Hamilton Straight has not only witnessed six of the seven home wins [at the time] achieved by Lewis but it has also been the scene of much euphoria as the passionate Silverstone fans gather here to join him to share the post-race celebrations. For many, the opportunity to walk on the hallowed tarmac after the British Grand Prix is one of the highlights of their race weekend experience.'

Coulthard commented, 'I was delighted, in my capacity as President of the BRDC, to share this news with Lewis today. It is the first time in Silverstone's history that a part of the circuit has been named after any individual. Lewis has become a huge part of this history and the directors of the Club and I felt there was no better way to mark this than to rename the iconic pits straight in recognition of his record-breaking achievements.'

Lewis's reign began in 2008, in torrential rain. In a race that tested the mettle of every driver, Hamilton delivered a masterclass in his McLaren, lapping all but two cars and finishing over a minute ahead. Even fellow podium finishers Nick Heidfeld and Rubens Barrichello were left trailing. Let's not forget, this was just his second season in F1; he was clearly a once-in-a-generation, no, a once-in-a-lifetime talent. His pace on intermediates, earned him the victory. It was the start of what, for many fans and pundits, heralded his prominence as F1's undoubted best driver ever in the rain.

He had started fourth on the grid, behind Heikki Kovalainen (pole), Mark Webber and Kimi Räikkönen. The track was treacherously slippery, with aquaplaning and poor visibility. Despite the dreadful conditions, Hamilton made a brilliant start, immediately jumping from fourth to second, and challenged teammate Kovalainen for the lead within the opening corners. He briefly fell back but kept up the pressure on Heikki, passing him at Stowe on lap five and taking the lead.

Hamilton would not relinquish it for the rest of the race, much to the delight of his thousands upon thousands of fans at his home GP. OK, he did have one scare – when the car took a 360° spin at Abbey – but he coolly kept it out of the barriers, and rejoined without losing position.

Afterwards, a euphoric Hamilton said it was 'my best win', but added, 'It was one of the toughest races I've ever done. This would definitely go down as my best win – not only because it was history and my home ground, but because I drove one of my best ever races.

'I want to dedicate this to my family because I've had some troubles over the last couple of weeks [in two earlier Grands Prix] and it's been really tough. But as always, your family are there when you need them.'

He admitted that one major motivation, as always when he races at Silverstone, was 'not to let the fans down'. The win meant Hamilton, at 23, was tied on points with Räikkönen and Massa at the head of the championship. He would go on to lift the trophy at the end of the season and acknowledge the importance of his Silverstone victory in boosting his confidence.

Hamilton's boss, McLaren managing director Martin Whitmarsh, had no doubt he had witnessed a genius at work in the swamp at Silverstone. Reporters asked him how good the drive was when compared with other top-drawer McLaren wins at the venue. He replied, 'It's up there, isn't it? I'm a lousy historian so I'm ducking the question, but only because in the euphoria of the moment you can be disrespectful to the great things of the past.

'How many people were really struggling out there today? He found grip that other people didn't find. He was driving within himself comfortably quicker than anyone else. It was an astonishing performance.'

Another interesting viewpoint came in 2025 – from the readers and team behind BBC TV's ever-popular motoring series, *Top Gear*. To mark 75 years of Silverstone, the *Top Gear* team hosted a fans' online special, to pinpoint the best ever race at the circuit.

Unsurprisingly, viewers nominated Hamilton's master-class in 2008, as *Top Gear* explained: '2025 marks 75 years since the first-ever Formula 1 World Championship race was held at Silverstone, and there have been some memorable follow-ups since then. In our latest Question of the Week, we wanted to find out which race stood out most for our readers.

'So, let's begin with a suggestion from the creatively named Teabag Towers: "2008, when Lewis Hamilton made everyone else look like amateurs in the wet. The margin between him and Nick Heidfeld in second place was over a minute when the chequered flag was waved. Only Heidfeld and Rubens Barrichello finished the race on the same lap as Hamilton; everyone else was a lap behind."

'Yep, we suspected '08 would get a strong vote of confidence. Mish Mash agreed: "Having been too young to know what F1 was, I only heard about this race a couple of years ago. Intrigued, I watched the replay and was in awe of Hamilton's ability to master such tricky conditions. And to win by over a minute, that's ridiculous. Not even Max Verstappen at his best could do that, and it's why I think Hamilton's the best."'

Looking back on the triumph, in 2023, Lewis had this to say about 2008: 'I remember just feeling nervous. It was raining, that means mistakes can happen and it's the worst thing when it happens at your home, Grand Prix particularly. I remember my brother Nicholas coming into my room and he was like, "Don't worry about this, bro; you've got this, this is your weather." I just felt so at one with the circuit, I knew exactly where the grip is, where to put my car, where not to put my car.

'The conditions were so tough because people were just aquaplaning off, particularly going into Abbey. I just remember every time I'd make it through and not go off, I would see the fans sitting in the rain stand up. I knew that they were with me right on the edge of their seat like I was on the edge of my seat. That was for me, at least to that point, the greatest race that I had ever done.'

It was the kind of performance that comes once in a generation – an emphatic declaration that greatness had arrived.

From that moment on, Silverstone became Hamilton's fortress. In 2019, he outmanoeuvred teammate Valtteri Bottas in a tactical duel. In 2020, he crossed the finish line on three wheels after a last-lap puncture – a moment etched into F1 folklore. And in 2021, he overcame controversy and a collision with Max Verstappen to seize victory. Finally, in 2024, when many had begun to write the final chapter of his career, Hamilton roared back to the top of the podium at Silverstone for a record-breaking ninth time, proving that legends never fade.

That 2021 race is worth a mention as it underlines the enormous courage, determination and conviction of Hamilton on the racetrack. The determination to remain a winner, even as the years started to add up. The championship battle between Hamilton and Max Verstappen had reached boiling point, and fans knew sparks were likely to fly at Silverstone.

From the moment the lights went out, you could have cut the tension with a knife. Hamilton, starting second, was aggressive from the get-go, determined not to let Verstappen's pole position translate into an easy lead. The two diced dangerously through the opening corners, wheel to wheel, neither willing to yield.

Then, at Copse corner, Hamilton darted to the inside, a bold move at one of the fastest corners in Formula 1. Verstappen held his line, refusing to back down. The result was inevitable: contact. Verstappen's Red Bull was sent hurtling into the barriers at speed. The Dutchman was out of the race, and the paddock was instantly divided. Was it a racing incident? A reckless lunge? A calculated risk?

The stewards handed Hamilton a ten-second penalty, but the Briton was undeterred. With the crowd roaring him on, he mounted a relentless charge, eventually overtaking Charles Leclerc in the closing laps to take victory. It was his eighth win at Silverstone, but this one felt different – more defiant.

Verstappen, meanwhile, was taken to hospital for pre-cautionary checks. Red Bull were furious, with team principal Christian Horner branding Hamilton's move 'desperate' and 'dangerous'. The fallout was fierce; the rivalry had officially turned personal.

But for Hamilton, the win was a statement. A reminder that he was still very much up for the fight.

That would be the case also in 2024, his last win at the nostalgic old track, and, as this book went to the printers, possibly his last ever at Silverstone . . . although, of course, with Lewis Hamilton, never say never. At 39 years old, Hamilton arrived at Silverstone with critics whispering that his best days were behind him. He hadn't won a race since 2021, and some had quietly begun to write his epilogue.

But Hamilton, ever the fighter, had other plans, especially as this would be his final race for Mercedes before he joined Ferrari. The race itself was a masterclass in resilience and racecraft. Starting from second on the grid, behind teammate George Russell, he battled through changing weather, strategic chaos and fierce competition from younger rivals like Lando Norris and Oscar Piastri. Rain came and went, tyres changed and positions shuffled. At one point, both McLarens surged past him, and it looked like the fairy tale was slipping away. But Hamilton dug deep. He timed his switch to slick tyres perfectly, undercutting Norris and retaking the lead.

What followed was vintage Lewis: calm under pressure, but an emotional drive that seemed powered by something more than fuel and engineering. It felt like the crowd's adrenaline was whooshing the boy home one more time. Verstappen loomed large in his mirrors, but Hamilton held firm, crossing the line to claim his record-breaking ninth win at Silverstone – more than any driver has ever achieved at a single circuit.

There were tears in his eyes after the race, of joy and of relief. He wasn't daft; he knew some in the sport had been writing him off. Now he had replied in the most impressive way; winning on home ground, once again. Hamilton, usually composed, couldn't hold the tears back. 'I can't stop crying,' he admitted, overwhelmed by the moment. In the paddock, even seasoned veterans were moved. His engineer Bono's voice cracked with emotion over the radio. His father, Anthony, watched on, pacing nervously until the final lap. And the crowd – tens of thousands draped in Union Jacks – roared as their home-town hero waved to them and told them he loved them.

Later, he said, 'I know, it's been since 2021 [since the last win]. Every day, [I'm] getting up trying to fight to train, to put my mind to the task and work as hard as I can with this amazing team – and this is my last British Grand Prix with the team, so I wanted to win this so much for them because I love them and I appreciate them so much.

'All the hard work they've been putting in all over these years. I'm forever grateful to everyone in this team – everyone at Mercedes, all of our partners and our incredible fans. I could see them lap by lap as I was coming around. There's just no greater feeling than to finish at the front here.

'It's so tough [to go without a win]. I think for anyone. The important thing is how you continue to get up and continue to dig deep, even when you feel like you're at the bottom of the barrel. I mean there's definitely been days between 2021 and here where I didn't feel like I was good enough to get back to where I am today, but the important thing is that I had great people around me, continuing to support me and my team.

'Every time I turn up and see them putting in the effort, it encourages me to do the same thing. Otherwise, my friends, when I see them around the world, they have been so supportive. A big, big thank you to everybody back at the factory, and everyone here. I love you guys, and God bless you.'

Yet Silverstone has always been about the future as much as the past, and in the last two years, a new star has emerged in Lando Norris. His first win at Silverstone in 2025 was a dream realised, a boyhood fantasy made real before a home crowd that had longed for a new hero. His calmness under pressure, his ability to manage chaotic weather and multiple safety cars, and his sheer joy at winning endeared him instantly to the fans.

Just as Hamilton's 2008 win had heralded a new era, Norris's triumph suggested that Britain's proud tradition of Silverstone champions was alive and well.

Silverstone's history with British drivers reads like a saga. Each generation has produced its own heroes: Clark, Surtees and Hill in the 1960s; Stewart and Hunt in the 1970s; Watson in the 1980s; Mansell, Hill, Herbert and Coulthard in the '80s and '90s; Hamilton dominating the 2010s and beyond; and now Norris stepping forward as the future, with George Russell surely not far behind.

Each victory carried its own mood story – Clark's smooth mastery, Graham Hill's determination, Mansell's fiery passion, Herbert's redemption, Hamilton's relentless dominance and Norris's youthful spark. Together, these moments have made Silverstone not just a circuit, but a symbol of British pride, a place where history is made, legends are crowned and generations of fans find their voice supporting their local heroes. As Old Trafford is known as the Theatre of Dreams for many football fans, so Silverstone is the Theatre of Dreams for all UK motor racing aficionados.

Lando's win in 2025 was a rich reward for his push to arrive at the very top of the sport. You could argue that it had been coming. The previous year, he had finished third on the podium behind Hamilton and Verstappen. And in 2023, he was second behind Max, and ahead of Lewis.

In the win, he had to overcome a Silverstone circuit

that veered between wet and dry. The race was chaotic – full of heavy rain and safety cars. Norris benefited from a ten-second penalty given to teammate Oscar Piastri for a safetycar infringement, allowing Lando to secure the win.

But in front of more than 150,000 fans, he had to wrestle with the weather, two safety cars and the weight of expectation to deliver. At the very start, the circuit was wet and slippery, and while a few gambled on slick tyres, Norris and the majority of the field opted for intermediates, expecting the rain to intensify. It did.

Early on, Norris found himself in the thick of the fight, getting past Max Verstappen as the Dutchman slid wide in the wet. Then, it seemed his teammate Piastri might steal the spotlight, storming past to seize the lead. Pit strategy quickly became decisive. McLaren attempted the tricky manoeuvre of 'double stacking' both their drivers for fresh tyres – it cost them precious seconds and nearly undid their early advantage.

The rain was relentless, and soon the safety car was deployed, neutralising the race as marshals cleared incidents.

When racing resumed, the chaos multiplied. Another incident forced the safety car back out, compressing the field once more. Verstappen, usually so unshakable, lost control at the restart and spun, tumbling down the order. Piastri, meanwhile, picked up a penalty for braking erratically behind the safety car, scuppering his own hopes. Through it all, Norris kept his cool.

As the track finally began to dry, strategy came back into play. Piastri's penalty left him vulnerable, and Norris pounced. With a decisive move, he took back control of the race. Behind him, Nico Hülkenberg surged from 19th on the grid to secure a fairy-tale podium, but the afternoon belonged to the man in papaya orange.

Crossing the line, Norris screamed into the radio as the grandstands erupted, Union Jacks waving wildly. It was his first win at Silverstone, McLaren's first at the circuit since 2008, and a 1-2 finish for the team on home soil. But afterwards, Lando admitted the race had been 'as stressful as you can get'.

He became the 13th British driver ever to win the British Grand Prix, and the first Brit – apart from Lewis Hamilton – to win at Silverstone since David Coulthard's win in 2000. It was also McLaren's first win at the track since Hamilton in 2008.

Afterwards, he couldn't stop grinning, telling reporters, 'I've joined a long list of pretty incredible winners who have won here in the past. Most of them are Lewis! But to join him and, from a British side, to continue the reign of the British here is pretty amazing. And just for the fans. The last two laps, looking up at the fans and seeing them on their feet and cheering – these are moments that no one really gets, none of you guys get to witness. This is something that I and very few others, especially Brits, get to witness. It's a very selfish moment, but it's one of the most special, the most incredible, because it's such a rare thing that someone gets to feel and to see and to witness.

'No tears. I tried, but no. I don't know. When I get emotional, I don't cry, I just smile. It's pure happiness. It's pure enjoyment of the moment that you're in. I wish I could cry because I think it looks better for pictures sometimes.'

After winning the previous race in Austria, he had high hopes that he might go on to win the drivers' title – although he accepted teammate Piastri would have a massive say in that. 'I think it's still just one race at a time. Obviously, I had a good race last weekend and we had a good battle, and we got close, and I was looking forward to another good battle. I give my credit to Oscar at the same time because he drove an extremely good race.

'It's two wins, but they've not come easy by any means. We've had good fights, but they're pretty strenuous, exhausting weekends because you're fighting for hundredths and thousandths, and you're fighting for perfection every session and I'm against some pretty good drivers. It takes a lot out of you, especially when you have a race like today.

'I've had two good weekends and, of course, I would love to continue that momentum, but it still requires more consistency. Two weekends doesn't mean anything other-wise. And I just need to keep it up and keep working hard.'

George Russell's Silverstone experiences do not match up to Hamilton's or Norris's in terms of victories – yet. At the time this book was written, he hadn't even graced the podium, his best result arriving in 2023 when he finished just outside, in fifth.

In 2025, he finished tenth after limping home in the Mercedes and a year earlier, he was forced out, having earlier led from pole. His debut in 2019 was inauspicious when he ended up 14th in the Williams.

After the 2025 disappointment, due to a mix-up over tyres, he told reporters, 'Everything just went wrong at every single point. I feel at the beginning, pitting to slicks was not a stupid decision as we knew it was going to be dry for 25 minutes. But we had 15 minutes' worth of Virtual Safety Car and that didn't allow us to warm the tyres; it didn't allow us to benefit from the gains when it was dry. By the end of that stint, we were five seconds a lap faster than the wet runners.

'Then, at the end, maybe I called to pit one or two laps early, but I wasn't expecting the hard tyre and of course then it all just went wrong. A really disappointing day; if you play it safe, you'll come home with a safe result and that's not really what we were going for. If you have a fast car, you can afford to do what you want, and you'll always find yourself in a good position. At the moment unfortunately we don't have that luxury.'

In 2024, George had high hopes after landing pole in qualifying, beating Hamilton (P2) and Norris (P3). It earned a place in the history books, too – a British 1-2-3 on the grid for the first time at Silverstone in F1 history. Russell beat Hamilton to pole position by 0.171 seconds with Norris, second to Russell after the first laps in the final session, 0.211secs off the pace after failing to complete his second lap.

It was George's first pole at the British GP, and he said, 'What a feeling. At the start of this year I don't think we could have even dreamt of being on pole here; 1-2 for me and Lewis, and Lando, it's just mega. It's down to these fans as well. They give us so much energy so thank you for that.

The car is feeling so good, it really came alive in qualifying and what a joy to drive around this circuit. We are riding this wave at the moment and I'm absolutely buzzing, but eyes on tomorrow, we've got a race to win and it's going to be tight with Lando, Max is going to be fast as well but I'm so excited right now.'

He felt he could pull off his first home win and that the crowd at Silverstone would be willing him on. 'The crowd always gives us so much energy, the three of us; I don't think Silverstone could have dreamt of three Brits in the top three. We love the support and can't wait for the race tomorrow.'

So, after all the build-up and high hopes, it was a demoralising comedown for Russell in the race itself. Mercedes told him on Lap 34 that he had to 'retire the car'. He was running in P4 at the time when it suffered a water system problem, basically a leak. George said, 'I had alarms on my steering wheel for some sort of water cooling failure. The car had been so good. I felt good. But obviously, it's a real blow to withdraw from any race, let alone a home Grand Prix, when we had the car to win. It was a long race; I struggled a bit around the damp patches. Really disappointed. Everything was under control at the beginning in the dry, then very challenging conditions in the damp. I started losing power and next thing I had to retire the car, so yeah, really disappointing. Gutting.'

Team boss Toto Wolff expressed his sympathy for Russell's plight: 'George was unfortunate today. He has been so strong recently and took a fantastic pole position yesterday. Sadly, we had to retire his car because of a water system issue. He would have likely been in a position to fight for the win, were it not for that.'

Mercedes' trackside engineering director, Andrew Shovlin, also found time to console George, saying he could 'hold his head high'. He added later, 'It was a difficult race for George. We were monitoring a cooling system on his car from the early laps and unfortunately that got to a stage where we had to retire the car.

'He can hold his head up high though. He put together a fantastic lap to take pole position and showed that he had the pace to control the race in stint one.'

George was down but still found time to praise teammate Hamilton for his remarkable 'comeback' victory – the one many pundits had felt would not be possible. George said, 'Congratulations to Lewis and the team though. He drove a great race and it's a fully deserved victory. We've both been pushing so hard to help the team develop the car and it's great to see that paying off.'

Typical of George's humility and innate decency, he also still had kind words for his engineers and the team as he truly did feel the car was improving by the week. 'We had the car, in normal dry conditions, to achieve a double. We are clearly back, and I think we will fight for victories more often now.'

And talking of decency, one particular race at Silverstone in 2022 will always be remembered for George Russell's selfless act of courage and human kindness. OK, George has never won at Silverstone and his results admittedly are a mixed bag. But whatever the future holds for him at the

Northamptonshire track, no one in F1 will forget what he did when Zhou Guanyu's Alfa Romeo flipped upside down and ended up lodged between the fencing and the barriers.

Pierre Gasly's Alpha Tauri had clipped Russell's left-rear wheel as they went three wide with Zhou on the opening lap. That sent Russell's Mercedes veering into Zhou's Alfa, causing the flip. George's Mercedes suffered a puncture and suspension issues and slowed to a stop. He didn't park right next to Zhou – he took his car off to the side, near the crash area.

Russell then immediately jumped out of his car and ran across to the accident scene to check on Zhou. By the time he reached the Alfa Romeo, Zhou was still trapped in the car, upside down and wedged between the barriers. Russell did not pull him out himself, but stayed nearby, trying to help, and beckoned the marshals over.

He then allowed them and the medical team to free poor Zhou. But because George left his car – and the marshals brought it back to the pits on a truck – he was not allowed to restart the race, even though he'd hoped to. Later, George explained the sequence of events like this: 'We'd taken a gamble starting on the hard tyres because I didn't do a good enough job in qualifying, and we were starting out of position. We felt like it was our best opportunity to fight for a podium today, and it was. But we knew it would have been very difficult on Lap 1 and it turned out to be extremely difficult.

'I couldn't get any temperatures on the tyres on the formation lap, and I just got swamped by all the cars and next thing I know, I got a touch from behind, [went] in the side of Zhou.

'I saw the race was red-flagged, so I knew it was safe to jump out. I wanted to go see if Zhou was OK and if I could have helped in any way. When I came back, I couldn't get the car turned on, but there was no reason why I shouldn't have been able to because the car was fine. I ran back to the team to check and when I came back, the car was on the flat bed already. I asked the marshal to make sure that they didn't pick the car up and as it turned out there was nothing wrong with the car bar a puncture.

'It's really frustrating because we had the pace to definitely come back through to P6 as a minimum. So many emotions . . . but glad to see that Zhou is doing OK. It's horrible to see an incident like that.'

The following year, George reflected on the accident, and his reaction, in more detail. 'When you see an incident like this, at the end of the day, there are only 20 Formula 1 drivers, and you know how it feels inside that cockpit,' he told Motorsport.com. 'Wearing three layers of clothing and helmet, gloves and boots, with a radio plug-in, with a drink bottle in your mouth – it's quite claustrophobic. When you see a car flying through the air, and land in a position, which is essentially trapped, that's a pretty horrendous place to be in. I was out of the race and when you are out of the race, your first thought is, "Can I help him in a way?" I guess, if I was in that position, I would want every single bit of help as soon as possible, because you don't know what is going to happen next, the car's going on fire or whatnot.

So, I guess that was probably more of a human reaction as opposed to a racing driver reaction.'

Zhou was lucky. He escaped uninjured and was given the all-clear at the medical centre the same day. He credited the halo device with saving his life – just as it had with Hamilton when Verstappen's car landed on top of his at Monza in 2021. Zhou told his fans, 'It was a big crash and I'm glad I'm OK. The marshals and the medical team at the track were fantastic with their quick response, and I also owe my thanks to the FIA and Formula 1 for all the work they have done, and they keep doing, to improve the safety of our cars.

'The Halo saved me today and it goes to show that every step we take in improving our cars has real, valuable results. I'm keener than ever to get back on track and do what I love: I'm fit and I'm looking forward to Austria next week.'

He also thanked Russell for his concern and sportsmanship.

Two years later, in Abu Dhabi, he exchanged helmets with George in Abu Dhabi, and once again paid tribute to the Englishman who had so selflessly come to his rescue at Silverstone. The Sauber driver wrote on Instagram, 'This moment in Silverstone, in 2022, I will always remember. Thank you, George.'

Zhou also revealed his gratitude when interviewed by talkSPORT in 2024. He said, 'I was just really grateful to see George do such a sportsmanlike gesture. Not just because we are friends but the way he was able to do it as he was involved in the incident too. He jumped out of his car to make sure I was OK. Keeping an eye on me and helping instruct the medical teams to get over there as quickly as possible. It gave me a really warm feeling. I'm grateful we fight on track the hardest we can, but we have huge respect for each other.'

IndyCar racer Callum Ilott also commented on Russell's actions – and revealed it hadn't been the first time he had helped out in such a way. On his Twitter (X) account, Callum said, 'The first time I flipped a go-kart, [George] stopped on track to lift it off of me. He's always been a good egg since day 1, a great role model for anyone.'

The incident summed up George the driver, and George the person. As a driver, he had still wanted to race on despite being involved in a horrific crash, and seeing what had happened to his friend, Zhou. That highlighted his bravery and ambition in F1.

As a person, he didn't overdramatise his actions afterwards – in fact, he downplayed his role. He made it clear that, in his eyes, the marshals and medical staff were the ones who really saved Zhou. That humility reinforced the impression of a genuinely decent, caring, compassionate man. While this chapter has rightly emphasised the stirring wins of Lewis Hamilton, Lando Norris and other Brit legends right back to Jim Clark at Silverstone, George Russell can stand proud, too, and tell of his own triumph at the legendary Northamptonshire track. He may not have won – yet as we keep saying – but his victory was wonderful in its own way: rushing towards danger without a second thought, to help save a fellow driver's life.

CHAPTER 7

A STAR IS BORN

By 21 August 2025, Hamilton, Norris and Russell had competed together in a total of 138 Formula 1 Grands Prix. The only time they haven't raced together was at Sakhir in 2020 – when Russell stood in for Covid-hit Hamilton at Mercedes. Otherwise, the trio have been testing each other on the track constantly since 2019. Out of those 138 Grands Prix, Lewis notched 31 wins, Lando nine and George four. It shows the relative success of each man over the past few years. In 2025, Lando was in the ascendancy, thanks to McLaren's powerful machine, George was coming up fast and Lewis was struggling to get to grips with his new Ferrari in Italy.

Lando took a while to break through, with his first win coming in 2024 after 110 race starts. By August 2025, he had racked up those nine as he made a strong claim for the season's drivers' title.

As a sidenote, he wasn't the only top driver to take a fair amount of time to scoop their first GP victory. Sergio Perez, for instance, took a staggering 190 races, Carlos Sainz 150, Mark Webber 130, Rubens Barrichello 124, Jenson Button 113 and Nico Rosberg 111. George Russell scored his maiden win at São Paulo in 2022. He added two more in 2024 (Austria and Las Vegas) and one in 2025 (Canada).

For Lewis, 2019 and 2020 were dominant seasons – 11 wins in each, including his seventh world title in 2020. The following year saw fierce competition with Verstappen, but Hamilton still bagged eight wins.

But the years 2022 to 2024 were leaner ones as Mercedes struggled with performance. His last win came at the 2024 Belgian Grand Prix.

Amid this plethora of stats, it's interesting to try to pinpoint which GP was arguably the standout one for each driver; which suggested they had arrived and would be a real threat for years to come? Obviously, the debate answer is debatable! But looking back through the mass of information and those 138 Grands Prix, it is possible to choose one for each of them.

In Hamilton's case, of course his win in Turkey in 2020, which secured his seventh world title, stands out.

But if we're looking for a race in which he not only announced himself as a contender, but a future champion, it was surely the Canadian GP in 2007. He took his maiden Formula 1 victory at the Circuit Gilles Villeneuve in Montreal. It was only his sixth race in F1, and he was just 22 years old, driving for McLaren Mercedes alongside

Fernando Alonso. He out-qualified teammate Fernando Alonso by nearly half a second. It was his first pole in Formula 1 – and he converted it into his first win, becoming the first black driver to win a Formula 1 Grand Prix.

He arrived in Montreal confident but a little weary after some sniping in the paddock. Statistically, he had done remarkably well. In the five races beforehand, he had finished third in Melbourne and followed up that debut with four second places – in Malaysia, Spain, Bahrain and Monaco. Those stats were unheard of for a rookie in the sport, yet some wisecrackers had apparently begun to dub him 'the bridesmaid' because of those runner-up spots. He had laughed it off and it was clearly the jibes of envious guys in other garages, but it added to a now-ridiculous level of pressure. The rookie was expected to start winning, after just five previous races . . .

By 10 June 2007, in Montreal, Hamilton's response was to turn up on Thursday to 'bed himself in' for a Sunday race at speeds of up to 203mph in front of a crowd pushing 105,000 on 70 punishing laps.

And, on Sunday afternoon, he would stand on the podium once again; for the sixth consecutive time, but the first as the winner. The 'bridesmaid' had eventually reached the altar.

Raceday brought ideal weather – mild, dry, sunny, not too hot.

Hamilton's pole had delighted team boss Ron Dennis, who said, 'A fantastic qualifying result for Lewis to achieve his first ever Formula 1 pole position. Fernando was unlucky on his second qualifying lap not to have improved following two great first sectors. We are confident that we will have a strong showing in tomorrow's race but certainly will not be complacent.'

Mercedes boss Norbert Haug, also a big backer of Hamilton, was similarly pleased for the Brit, saying: 'Lewis will start from his first Formula 1 pole position in only his sixth Grand Prix. Fernando was fastest in both the first and second sectors and until the final sector it looked like he would make it. Lewis and Fernando achieved the best possible qualifying result for the team for the second time within a fortnight.'

The Circuit Gilles Villeneuve is often described as technically 'simple' by the drivers – yet it has produced some of the most chaotic, memorable races. The day Hamilton came of age was no different. The race was hit by four safety car interventions, including a terrifying crash involving Robert Kubica, whose BMW slammed into the wall at nearly 150mph. Miraculously, he escaped with only a sprained ankle and concussion. Lewis's teammate Alonso was off form that day, making multiple errors and finishing seventh.

Amid the chaos, a newcomer to F1 might have been forgiven for losing focus. But Hamilton was no ordinary rookie. He kept his cool through every restart, showed maturity beyond his years, and led the field with commanding pace. Lewis led the majority of the 70 laps and crossed the line in 1:44:11.292 – 4.340 seconds ahead of second-placed Nick Heidfeld.

Making his way up to the podium, Lewis headed straight

for Ron Dennis, gave him a bear hug and ran up the steps and out on to the podium to celebrate. He said he was 'over the moon' as he savoured the sweet taste of victory: 'I've been ready for the win for quite some time. It was just a matter of when and where. I have to dedicate this win to my dad because without him, this would not have been possible.'

He added. 'I didn't make a great getaway. Fernando got a better start and I had to make sure I didn't leave a gap for Nick behind me. Then I saw Fernando come flying down the outside and thought, oh no, I'm going to lose the lead, but he just went straight on at the corner. I continued on my line and got a fantastic exit, and then Fernando came cutting across in front of me. It was pretty exciting!'

He continued, 'I'm on another planet after this – I simply can't find the words to describe what it feels like to win my first Formula 1 race. The team has done a fantastic job and I'm so happy to be part of the Vodafone McLaren Mercedes family. It seemed like every time I opened up a bit of a gap, the safety car came out and I had to start all over again. It was only a few laps from the end [that] I realised that victory was within my grasp and I started noticing things like the fans cheering, and when I crossed the finishing line it was amazing.

'It's been an incredible start to my Formula 1 career.'

Lewis was also asked what dad Anthony had said to him directly after the race. He stumbled for a second, emotion almost getting the better of him, then replied, 'I haven't seen him [to talk to] but obviously I could see him in the crowd while I was on the podium and it looked like he had a tear in his eye. So, it's obvious that he was extremely proud and you wouldn't believe the amount of work he's put into my career. He had nothing when he was younger – just to see his family be successful is a real pleasure to him.'

Anthony too was choked up when told his son had dedicated the win to him. 'I hadn't heard that,' he said. 'But I'm glad I didn't hear it because who knows what would have happened? I was trying to hold it back as it was. This was the ordinary guy who makes good. It's a special day for us but also for lots of other people, Formula 1 people and not Formula 1 people.'

Ron Dennis added his own tribute after Lewis's 'mature and disciplined drive', saying, 'It's been a very long time since the British national anthem was played for a race winner. His family should be justifiably proud of his achievement and whatever McLaren and Mercedes-Benz have contributed only complements his talent and commitment. Lewis has done a great job; he deserved it and I am happy for him.'

Back home, the tributes poured in as the night progressed. Sir Stirling Moss said of the young man who had become the 19th British driver to win a Grand Prix: 'He is a very impressive young man, the most impressive young driver I've seen in a long while. He has the car control and he has calmness when he is driving, but he is also a fighter and has a great manner about him. He'll go a long way. I was impressed with him at the beginning of the season, but even more so now. It was obvious how good he was, but I never thought – and I don't think anybody thought – he would be leading the World Championship.

'For a guy who has just come into the sport, that is unbelievable, so I am terribly impressed and what has impressed me more than anything is that he is a racer.'

Another great Brit, Sir Jackie Stewart, went even further, saying: 'He is probably the brightest star that has entered Formula 1 – ever!'

And Sir Frank Williams said, 'He is absolutely a brilliant driver. You could almost describe him as a phenomenon, given that he is achieving so much with no Formula 1 experience. He is very, very remarkable.'

Damon Hill made a prediction that would turn out to be uncannily correct: 'People should not underestimate what he has achieved in an incredibly short space of time. He may be young and in his first season, but this guy is the real deal. If you're good enough in this sport, you're old enough – and, boy, is Lewis good enough!

'He's leading the World Championship and winning races, so his confidence will be sky-high. And he's shown he can handle the pressure. We shouldn't get too carried away, but we could be looking at the next British world champion.'

F1 fans back in Blighty celebrated long into the night, confident that they had not only seen history made on their TV sets, but that they had witnessed the dawn of a new epoch in the sport: the dawn of the Lewis Hamilton era. This is why Canada in 2007 was not only Hamilton's vital first win; it was much more than that. It filled him with the confidence that he could not only go on to eventually secure a first world title, but he could do it many times. If he had the talent to already beat the best as a rookie, imagine what he would do with more experience. It was the win that opened up a world he would ultimately dominate.

For Lando Norris, his first win in F1 would also be a momentous moment, career-defining in that it pumped up his self-belief and proved to doubters that he too could thrive at the highest level of the sport – and that he was worthy of a top machine to try to achieve his aim of being number one. It also finally put a lid on the horrible comments on social media framed around him taking 110 races to finally secure victory. Fans had nicknamed him 'Lando No Wins' and the term had become ever present around the circuit. The press even acknowledged it, although Lando, to his absolute credit, smiled when told of it and joked about it. But it wasn't much fun having his talent and skills consistently questioned so the victory was truly a weight off his still young shoulders. He had been 19 years and four months old when he started in his first GP and was 24 years and five months when he won in Miami.

Former F1 champ Nico Rosberg had also been critical, although he would claim it was constructive criticism, saying Lando had a psychological flaw that needed addressing. He said, 'I don't know if Lando has a mental coach. Does he work with a psychologist or not? He definitely should because there's so much value in that.

'I worked with one, just to help understand the best possible approach. I did two hours every two days leading up to the season. It was more difficult than the physical training. It was insanely difficult and extremely valuable.'

On another occasion, Rosberg advised that constant

negativity – even self-directed – can be damaging, 'If you say every day that I'm not good enough, at some point you'll believe it . . . I would strongly recommend that he reduces that, not always the negative.'

Irrespective of the criticisms, it wasn't as if the win hadn't been coming. Lando's form was good and he could even have taken top spot at the 2021 Russian GP, where he came agonisingly close but was denied by late rain and a critical pit-stop decision. McLaren and Norris decided to stay out on slick tyres despite worsening conditions. Hamilton switched to intermediates when Mercedes called him in; a clever decision. The rain intensified quickly. Norris lost grip, ran wide, and Hamilton swept past with only a few laps remaining. It proved to be Lewis's 100th career F1 victory. Lando came home in seventh, having taken on the intermediates far too late.

'I don't know where to start. I'm unhappy, devastated in a way,' he told Sky Sports F1 afterwards. 'We made a call to stay out and we stand by that. It was the wrong one at the end of the day but I made the decision just as much as the team. It was more that they thought I should box and I decided to stay out.

'I thought it was the way to go. The team told me what was going on and I said I want to stay out, so it's not the team's fault. I made my decisions and they told me it was only going to be drizzling like it was for those first five laps, but it rained a lot more. That's something we didn't know for some reason; Mercedes seemed to know it was going to rain a lot more; it's something I'll talk to the team about.'

McLaren team principal Andreas Seidl added, 'In hind-sight, it's always easy to judge what we could've done differently. We didn't get it together as a team in hindsight; it was the wrong decision to stay out, but it's part of the sport. Lando is long enough in this sport now to know it's part of the game, part of the learning. But not just on his side, but on the team side as well because I think there is always a chance to overrule him from the pit wall side with the information we are having. In the end, together we made this call to stay out. We wanted to go for the win; that's why we decided together to stay out and it just didn't work out.'

In Miami, on 5 May 2024, there was no rain and no mistakes, and certainly no anguish at a bad call. No, all went to plan and there was only joy that after 110 starts and 15 podium finishes, Miami was where the long wait finally ended. There had been signs in the previous three races – he'd finished third in Australia, fifth in Japan and runner-up in China, the last outing before Miami.

Lando had never really set the circuit alight on previous occasions in Miami. Situated in Miami Gardens, Florida, around the Hard Rock Stadium, home to the Miami Dolphins NFL team, the track winds through the stadium complex, giving it a unique 'stadium atmosphere' with fans surrounding the action. But while the fans enjoy the close involvement, the drivers aren't always as enthusiastic.

'It's probably at the bottom of my list of preferred circuits,' Lewis Hamilton told motorsport.com. Fernando Alonso added, 'I think the part of the track from Turn 12 to 15 is probably not really made for these Formula 1 cars, but it's the same for everybody. You just try to survive that sector but it's not really a sector where you can push or find a tenth of a second or something like that, you just go in the middle of the track and it's not super interesting.'

No matter, it was the track where Lando Norris would make personal history. He did not begin the race from pole; he started fifth on the grid. Pole setter Max Verstappen, as so often, was the early favourite. The McLaren team, however, had arrived in Miami with confidence. They brought a major upgrade package, including changes to the front wing, suspension and aerodynamics. These upgrades showed promise in practice and qualifying. Norris himself admitted afterwards, 'I feel like we've had many opportunities. We've been getting closer and closer. We've never been able to put it all together but today was that day.'

The early stages of the race were all about keeping calm. Norris held position and maintained pace, avoiding mistakes on a track known for its tricky grip levels. The turning point came when a safety car was deployed on lap 29 following a crash involving Kevin Magnussen and Logan Sargeant. It allowed Norris to pit and emerge ahead of Verstappen, who had already pitted under green flag conditions.

From there, it became about composure under pressure. Verstappen rarely lets a lead slip without a fight, and the reigning world champion loomed large in Norris's mirrors. But the Briton did not falter. Lap after lap he kept control, and the McLaren held its pace all the way to the flag.

Verstappen had struggled with floor damage and couldn't match Norris's pace. Norris finished 7.6 seconds ahead of him.

After crossing the line, Lando's voice over the team radio was filled with emotion as he celebrated with the crew that had been behind him since his debut. He told them, 'I love you all, I love you all. Thank you so much. We did it, Will! We did it! I guess that's how it's done. Finally, I'm so happy. I knew it. I knew it as I came in this morning. I said, "Today is the day; what an opportunity." I nailed it, you nailed it. Thanks, Mum, thanks, Dad, this one is for my grandma. Thank you very much.'

Later, he added, 'About time! What a race. It's been a long time coming, but finally I've managed to do it. I'm so happy for my whole team, I finally delivered for them. A long day, tough race, but finally on top, so I'm over the moon.

'I've made a lot of mistakes over the last five years in my short career, but today we put it all together. This is all for the team. I stuck with McLaren because I could believe in them and do believe in them. Today we proved exactly that.'

Referring back to the unkind 'Lando No Wins' nickname, he also admitted he was glad to finally consign that to the past. 'I never lost faith, I never didn't believe in what I could go out and do,' Norris said. 'So happy to put that to bed and prove a lot of these people wrong.

'I like all the comments of people abusing me. I freaking love it; it makes me smile more than anything, especially "Lando No Wins". For me to finally prove those people wrong and prove to people that didn't think I could go out and do it, it puts an even bigger smile on my face today. So, I thank all of them.'

It was McLaren's first win since the Italian GP at Monza in 2021, so not just a key date in Lando's world. It also meant so much to the team as they continued to move forward with the cars. 'This is long overdue,' McLaren CEO Zak Brown said post-race. 'I think this is a very popular win among the fans, among the drivers . . . look at how many drivers went up to him and congratulated him. He drove perfectly; the car was really fast. So proud of this team. Andrea, Lando, Oscar and all the men and women at McLaren have done an awesome job; this is just the start.'

Even Max Verstappen had kind words for Lando – although that's not as surprising as it may sound. Max can be harsh on many drivers, or simply non-committal, but he counts Norris as a friend, if not his best friend on the circuit. Max said, 'If I get beaten, it's great that it has been done by Lando. He deserves it. It's been a long time coming and it's going to be the first of many. Maybe it's also a bit of relief for him that he has that win now; who knows what's going to happen next?

'But for sure they had a strong weekend. Maybe it was a little bit messy still [in qualifying], but today they were flying – and especially Lando was flying. So definitely very happy for him.'

Another pal of Lando, Charles Leclerc, also got in on the congratulations. 'I'm really happy for him. As much as we all want to beat each other and to come out on top, it's always emotional to see so many emotions in one of your competitors. We have all grown up together. Max and I were in the same category but you always keep an eye on the younger categories.

'I remember looking at Lando, when we all had the same dream of being a Formula 1 driver one day. Then once you achieve that you obviously want the first win. I remember my first win and it is a very, very special moment. I told him already that he needs to enjoy it as much as possible. He definitely deserves it.'

Fellow Brit George Russell added, 'Obviously happy to see Lando finally get a victory. It seemed well deserved. He has done an amazing job for a long time. It was always when, not if, mate. Congrats, you deserve it.'

And finally, Lewis Hamilton also got in on the act, telling Sky Sports, 'I'm really happy for Lando. It's such a special moment to win your first Grand Prix. I started at McLaren and I'm really happy to see them back at the top. It's been a long time. I just told him he needs to stay [in Miami] tonight [to celebrate]! He's going to try and change his flight. He's got to! He just won a race.'

Finally, before the party started and went on late into the night, Lando paid tribute to the support his family had given him and told why he had dedicated the win to his grandmother. He said, 'My parents have been so supportive; they're the ones who are with you from the start. They allowed everything to happen. They're the ones that got me into racing, supported me, and allowed me to get to Formula 1, reach my dream, and do what I've loved to do since I was a kid. My grandma, because she's not been so well lately. I saw her last week and I told her that I was going to win a race. I didn't say when, I just said I was going to win a race. I didn't think it would be coming this soon, so I'm just very happy that I was able to do it as quickly as I did.'

His words of thanks echoed those by Hamilton after he won his first F1 race. Both men knew that without their support – and their respective fathers in particular – this ultimate triumph in motorsport wouldn't have been likely. The families came from different parts of the spectrum in terms of finances and prestige, but both had delivered for their sons via hard graft, dedication and cash to keep the dream alive. While Hamilton's dream had arrived in Canada in 2007, Lando had truly accomplished his own American dream by securing victory in Miami. The Miami Grand Prix of 2024 was the day Lando Norris broke through the barrier that had defined the early years of his career, and the day he could finally call himself a Formula 1 race winner.

In the case of our third Great Briton, I'd argue that George Russell's standout race, the one that defined his career, wasn't his first win in Brazil in 2022, but his first race for Mercedes in Sakhir in 2020. Of course, I'm not decrying in the least the acclaim and momentum that win brought for George. He beat teammate Hamilton to the top spot, after successfully keeping him in his mirror – the apprentice had finally mastered the master. It was also the first time two British drivers had finished a Grand Prix first and second since Hamilton and Jenson Button at the 2010 Canadian Grand Prix.

After watching Lewis for years, from a distance and then close up, and learning from his brilliant drives and engineering and tactical know-how, George now put it all together to come home first. He beat Lewis by 1.5 seconds in São Paulo, chalking up Mercedes' first GP win of the season.

The win left him in tears, as he admitted from inside the car to the team. 'I need some tissues,' he said. 'I am crying, boys and girls. It has been an emotional roller coaster . . . Lewis put me under so much pressure. This is just the beginning.'

He dominated from the start, after taking the Saturday sprint – and became the first British driver to hear 'God Save the King' played for the race winner after the death of Queen Elizabeth II on 8 September and the accession of King Charles III.

So, given the power of the win, and the importance of it historically, it's certainly in the top two in terms of George's career advancement.

It certainly meant a lot to Mercedes. The team were quick to highlight its importance in their history as they devoted a section to the win on their official website. Titled, That Winning Feeling: Brazil 2022, it commented further, 'A moment he would have dreamed of from the second he first stepped into a go-kart. When George lifted the trophy on the top step of the podium on Sunday afternoon in São Paulo and took the applause of the team and the adoring Brazilian fans below, you could see from his eyes that it was mission accomplished.

'He was a Formula 1 race winner, and it was nothing more than he deserved. Having cruised home on Saturday afternoon to take the flag first in the F1 sprint, he again showed a level of maturity and precision beyond his years on Sunday, holding off Max Verstappen, both Ferraris and seven-time champion teammate Lewis Hamilton to claim his maiden victory.

'The result was the catalyst for an outpouring of emotion. But this was just pure happiness. There was even time for a quick FaceTime with the boss, with Toto dialling in from home to congratulate his latest Mercedes F1 Grand Prix winner.'

After the victory, a delighted George said, 'What an amazing feeling. A huge thank you to the whole team for making this possible. It's been an emotional roller coaster, this season, this race. I felt in control. Lewis was super-fast and then when I saw the safety car, I thought this is going to be a difficult end.

'He put me under so much pressure, but I'm so happy to come away with the victory. On the in-lap, all of these memories came flooding back, starting off with my mum and dad in go-karting, going through and all the support I've had from the rest of my family, my girlfriend, my trainer, my manager. The likes of Gwen, who first gave me the opportunity to get on the programme with Mercedes, and James Vowles and Toto. I can't thank everyone enough.'

Lewis was quick to congratulate him on the team's website, 'I have to say huge congratulations to George; what an amazing drive he did today. He also did an amazing job yesterday in the Sprint so he truly deserves it. To my Team, I'm so proud of everyone back at the factory and here. This is an incredible result – we've worked so hard through this year to get a 1-2, and to get a win. This is hugely, hugely deserved for everybody, so a big thank you to you all!'

But the 2020 race was just as vital, albeit in a different way, as two years earlier, it had catapulted him into F1 top-drawer attention and led to his becoming a full-time driver for Mercedes. It was also a remarkable debut, and only a couple of cruel mishaps deprived George of claiming what would have been a stunning victory while a mere rookie.

Russell was called up late by Mercedes to step in for Hamilton, who had been hit by Covid-19. ESPN explained the intricacies of the deal between Mercedes and Williams that allowed it to go ahead: 'Williams, which is an engine customer of Mercedes, agreed to release the 22-year-old for this weekend's race and has announced it will replace Russell with its reserve driver, Jack Aitken.

'Russell has a contract with Williams until the end of 2021, but is managed by Mercedes and has a separate long-term deal with the world champions. When news broke of Hamilton's positive test on Monday, Mercedes approached Williams over Russell's availability and once a deal was struck, the two teams confirmed the driver switch on Wednesday morning.'

Russell knew this was his big chance and was indebted to Williams for allowing him to take it. He said, 'I want to say a huge thank you to everybody at Williams for giving me this opportunity. I might be wearing a different race suit this weekend, but I'm a Williams driver and I'll be cheering my team on every step of the way.

'I see this as a great chance to learn from the best outfit on the grid right now and to come back as an improved driver, with even more energy and experience to help push Williams further up the grid. A big thank you also to Mercedes for putting their faith in me. Obviously, nobody can replace Lewis, but I'll give my all for the team in his absence from the moment I step in the car. Most importantly, I wish him a speedy recovery.'

Mercedes team boss Toto Wolff was also keen to express his gratitude to Williams for helping out in a crisis, 'I wish to thank our loyal partners at Williams for their collaboration and open-mindedness in making it possible for George to race for Mercedes this weekend. The conversations with the team at Williams were positive and pragmatic, and those were the key factors in reaching an agreement.'

Wolff accepted that it was a risk, in that George wouldn't have had time to accustomise himself with the car or the team. He was going into the unknown but Toto felt pretty confident he could handle the situation. 'It will not be a straightforward task for George to make the transition from the Williams to the W11, but he is race-ready and has detailed understanding of the 2020 tyres and how they perform on this generation of cars. George has shown impressive form this year with Williams, playing an instrumental role in their climb up the grid, and I am optimistic that he will deliver a strong performance alongside Valtteri [Bottas], who will be a demanding reference for him.

'This race will mark a small milestone for us as we see a member of our junior programme compete for the works Mercedes team for the first time. We have a job to do this weekend, and the full focus of our sporting efforts will be behind Valtteri and George in order to maximise our points score as a team. But, of course, our thoughts are also with Lewis, and we will be supporting him as much as we can to make a rapid recovery during his period of self-isolation.'

George would later relate how it came about, and how it all turned into a type of madcap race to set it up; it was as if the race itself was a minor afterthought, such were the obstacles to be overcome for him to get in the car in the first place. He told Sky Sports F1: 'I got a phone call from Toto at 2am on Tuesday morning. I was actually in the bathroom, which was slightly awkward.

'So, I answered the phone and he said, "George, are you in the bathroom?" I was like, "Yeah, sorry I am in the bathroom!" He said, "Unfortunately, Lewis has caught Covid. He's doing well, is healthy and feels fine," which is the most important, but then, "We want you to drive."

'So, I'm incredibly thankful to Mercedes for putting their faith and belief in me because there was a lot of work that went into making it happen. Logistically, getting helmets painted, getting suits made, lawyers working through the night to write contracts, amendments to Williams contracts . . . you know, it was chaos for 24 hours. I had 64 phone calls in the day back and forth between everybody!'

There was also the problem of actually fitting into the car as he was much taller than Hamilton, and bigger.

He admitted, 'Fitting into it is one way of putting it! Do I squeeze in? I do squeeze in. The biggest issue is actually my feet – I've got size 11 feet. Lewis and Valtteri [Bottas] have smaller feet so I'm actually wearing one size smaller boots than I would do originally.

'Not the most comfortable but I'm sure I can endure the pain . . . only through the 87 laps on Sunday!'

George appeared very laid-back and sanguine about the opportunity that had arisen from nowhere. There had already been suggestions that he might have been lined up as a potential teammate for Hamilton for the following season, at the expense of Bottas. So, in the minds of some pundits – and fans – this would be an ideal chance for him to lay down a marker for that role. But when asked at a press conference if he viewed it that way, he gave the idea short shrift.

He said, 'There have been no targets expected of me by Mercedes as you can't judge somebody off one race. It's not at the back of my mind [the possibility of replacing Bottas]. I'm going to go out there, enjoy it and learn as much as I can. I have a job to do on my return to Williams – to try to push that team forward. I need to take this opportunity with both hands and maximise the learning. The future will be judged over the course of a season, and what's happened in the past, not just one or maybe two races.'

George had been Mercedes' reserve driver in 2017 and 2018, but hadn't driven the newer car. He admitted, 'I am being thrown in at the last opportunity. I haven't driven their simulator in two years. My seat is three years old. I have so much information to learn and going up against Valtteri isn't going to be easy. Valtteri has been pushing Lewis an incredible amount.

'When you are integrated in a team, changing suddenly, there are so many new things to learn. I have no expectations, no targets. I am in a good position. I am not putting any additional pressure on myself. I am going to go out and enjoy it. This weekend will be all about learning, especially Friday.'

Bottas, always a decent, humble and likeable man, and a reliably consistent driver, was more than generous in his analysis of what might happen on the track, 'If he beats me, for sure it wouldn't look so good on me if I had a normal race, so I'll try to avoid that! But I'm not a person who thinks like that. I try to turn things into motivation and positive thinking and that's my mindset for this weekend.'

Hamilton wished George the best of luck, and felt sure he would do well in the race. For his own part, in missing out, he wrote on social media, 'I am devastated I won't be racing this weekend. Since we started the season in June my team and I have been taking all the precautions we possibly can [for Covid] and following the regulations everywhere we have been in order to stay safe. I am gutted not to be able to race but my priority is to follow the protocols and advice to protect others. I am really lucky that I feel OK with only mild symptoms and will do my best to stay fit and healthy.'

As he climbed into the Mercedes, George was determined to make a big impression. He had yet to earn a point in F1, but had been impressive in qualifying that season and had finished 11th once and 12th twice in his F1 career. Not that successful but, as we have previously noted, that was never due to his talent, or ability in the car; it was a result of operating in a car that wasn't the fastest or among the fastest. A car that needed major upgrading if it were to compete with the likes of the Mercedes and the Red Bulls.

Despite it being his first outing in the car, he immediately got up to speed, topping FP1 and FP2, and qualifying on the front row alongside Valtteri Bottas. In FP1, he was 0.176 seconds quicker than Verstappen while Bottas was fourth, 0.322secs off the pace. The Finn made a series of mistakes on his laps and damaged his car in an off-track moment at Turn 8. In FP2, Russell again topped the time sheets with a lap of 54.713secs.

Afterwards, he said, 'I do think the lap times are a little bit deceiving at the moment and aren't a true representation of our pace. I thought FP2 was not a great session for me. I struggled, especially on high fuel, and ultimately that's going to be key on Sunday. So, I still have a lot of work to do to get comfortable in the car, get comfortable with the set-up and make some improvements, because I think tomorrow is going to be a different story.'

He had done brilliantly but admitted 'a lot of hard work' had gone into the early success – and that he was still learning about the car. 'There is so much to take in, to learn. Lap after lap I'm just learning more and more. I'm doing my absolute best to be as prepared as possible, but jumping in the car with a day and a half notice is tricky. I'm doing my best; it was a good first day but there's definitely work to be done.

'Race starts are OK. They are improving. They are not Lewis Hamilton level to say the least, but they are getting better. So, loads of practice tonight sat in the car, trying and trying and modifying clutch pedals to try to suit my fingers a bit more. Like I say, there is so much I need to get on top of in a short period of time to do that. I think we're in for a long night.'

But he paid tribute to the engineers and the rest of the team at Mercedes. 'The driving style I was doing in the Williams last week, where I was strong last week in the Williams, was not working, and it was very different to Valtteri, very different to what Lewis was doing. I think the Mercedes just has so much more grip and so much more front end on the entry phase that could allow me to carry a bit more speed, but it was difficult.

'It's just a very different way to drive the car. I've been so impressed with the engineers I'm working with, how they've tried to show me how to improve. The standard of that team is absolutely incredible. They've really helped me to improve on the small things. Still not there yet, obviously, it's a strange track, only a day in the car but yeah, happy.'

The long hours paid off. In Q3, he finished just two-hundredths of a second behind Bottas to earn a front-row spot on the grid for the race, alongside his Mercedes teammate. Bottas had taken pole on his final Q3 lap with a time of 53.377secs, and Verstappen was third in the Red Bull. George revealed Lewis had wished him well for Sunday's race, 'Lewis dropped me a message on Friday night wishing me well and asking me to look after his car and so far, so good. It would be amazing to stand on the podium but as a racer you just want to deliver the best performance possible.'

Well, Russell did just that. He even led the race early on and looked destined for a remarkable victory until cruel fate struck. George suffered a pit-stop blunder and a puncture late on, which meant he finished ninth. That was a disappointment, of course, in terms of what might have been – but he had scored his first F1 points and had shown he was more than able to hold his own in the top realms of the sport.

Mercedes' own website summed up the significance of what had been an unexpected outing in Sakhir for Russell: 'George has been part of our Junior Programme since his GP3 career in 2017. In the same year, he undertook his first test with our Team in Hungary. Three years later, whilst at Williams, he was called up to make his Mercedes debut. This came at the 2020 Sakhir Grand Prix in Bahrain as he filled in for Lewis Hamilton, who was forced to miss the race, having contracted Covid-19.

'George was straight on the pace. Quickest in FP1 and FP2, he qualified on the front row alongside teammate Valtteri Bottas for Sunday's race. By Turn 2, he was in the lead.'

It was an advantage he wouldn't relinquish until a pit stop mishap following a late race safety car and a cruel puncture dropped him back to P9 at the flag. His first points in F1 were little consolation for what could have been so much more that night in Bahrain.

'I hope we get this opportunity again,' he said, in an audibly dejected post-race radio message to the Team.

He would. It had been a superb performance, and George had demonstrated to the watching world and F1 paddock what he was capable of in a car that could challenge for race wins.

The pit-stop incident occurred when he was forced to make an additional one after having the wrong tyres fitted during the Lap 62 pit. It cost him the lead. After climbing back to P2, George suffered a left-rear puncture that forced a further stop and eventually battled his way back to P9, scoring a further point for fastest lap.

Afterwards, George was, unsurprisingly, caught between two sets of emotions – pride that he had shown the world what he was capable of in a top car, but disappointment at losing out on what could have been. In a press conference, he admitted, 'I don't quite know how to sum up the mixture of emotions I'm feeling at the moment.

'On the one hand, I am proud of the job we did this weekend. I had a great group of people around me who worked very hard and diligently to get me prepared and ready for qualifying and the race.

'But today was absolutely gutting. I've had races before where I had a victory taken away from me, but it felt like that happened twice today; I still can't quite believe it. I had everything under control after the start and was managing the race, looking after my tyres and keeping the gap to Valtteri. Then we had that mess-up during the pit stop; I think there were some issues with the comms. That put us on the back foot, but I think we still could have won. And then the car was starting to feel a bit funny.

'I didn't want to believe it was a puncture. I just wanted to power through, but that obviously was not an option. I'm gutted, but also proud of what we have achieved and very happy to have had the opportunity to drive this car this weekend.'

Bottas, who finished a place above him in eighth, was very generous in his praise for his young teammate, saying, 'George had a good start and could control the race from there. The beginning of my second stint looked quite promising, my pace was good and I started making up time on George. Without the safety car, I think George and I would have ended up having a nice battle towards the end.

'George did a great job today and was just really unfortunate – I think he could have otherwise won this race.'

Team boss Wolff was also keen to praise the new boy, but as team bosses do, was more direct in his assessment of the blunders and the outcomes. In other words, he was critical, too: 'Overall, we messed up in a major way today. Obviously, it was looking good for us until the safety car was running. [We were] in a strong 1-2, we were fine on the hard tyres and could have stayed out, but we had the gap for a free stop and we took that opportunity. I think it was absolutely the right call, but it was a late one and we had a radio problem, which meant we didn't have the right tyres in the box. Which is why George exited with the wrong tyres and Valtteri left the pits on the same tyres he'd arrived with.

'Then we had to pit George again to correct the mistake. By then, the race was not lost and he battled back in an impressive way; but then he had the slow puncture and that dropped him back. These things can happen but obviously we need to investigate the problems, learn from them and move forward.

'It was heartbreaking for George after a monumental drive in his first race with Mercedes and he should have won. It didn't work out today, but I'm sure this isn't going to be his last attempt to win a race.'

The boss was absolutely correct in that prediction. The race definitely announced Russell's arrival on the big stage – his pace and composure under pressure prompted widespread acclaim and marked him out as a driver to watch.

A week later, George had to return to his back-of-the-grid Williams. 'To be honest, it felt strange to go back,' he told Speed Week. 'Before the Bahrain weekend, I really wanted to be able to contest the two races for Mercedes. I would then have taken the first weekend as a lesson and had no more excuses in Abu Dhabi.

'But the guys at Williams gave me this chance in Formula 1, working so hard for me over the past two years. It is my duty to do my best for them.'

That performance, stepping in for a champion in a top team, leading the race, and only being undone by unfortunate circumstances instantly marked Russell out as one to watch and defined his early Mercedes legacy.

CHAPTER 8

TECHNIQUE

When Lewis Hamilton is under starter's orders, his opening car stance differs from many drivers. While others have both hands on the steering wheel, he keeps just his left hand there. He then operates the clutch paddle with his other hand. The move is to gain a competitive edge by allowing for faster clutch releases, but also to limit the risk of an accidental downshift.

It is just one unusual aspect of his particular driving technique and style; one that sets him apart from many others. Hamilton has often said that he knew early on in his career that it wouldn't be enough to be simply a driver. If he wanted to win titles, he felt he had to be an engineer or one of his pits staffers. He needed to know everything there was to know in terms of technical and mechanical expertise. That way, he would have an edge on others in the car as it would provide the answers to what might be needed in any situation as he hurtled around the track at 200mph.

In this chapter, we will focus on the technique and styles favoured by Hamilton, Norris and Russell, and how they converge, or diverge from each other.

George has readily admitted that watching Lewis as a teammate, and seeing how he handled and got the best out of the Mercedes, was crucial to his own development. He learned from the master, and readily admitted it. 'From my experience, I can say that I learned more in my first year alongside Lewis than in the three years at Williams.' As well as showing obvious respect, it highlights George's humility in his willingness to listen and heed advice.

After their first season together, in 2022, George elaborated further on the valuable information and tips Lewis had imparted. 'I feel very fortunate to be in this team, a teammate of Lewis, learning a huge amount and being pushed to my limits,' he told *The High Performance Podcast*. 'It's not easy being teammates with somebody as fast and great as he is.'

'There have been a huge amount of late nights throughout this season, a lot of tension at times between drivers, teams, designers with regards to are we on the right track – do we need to be doing something different, more drastic? These were very difficult conversations, but we come away from them growing closer together.

'Lewis is an incredibly unique character. He's incredibly inspiring. He does things so differently to so many other people yet has still had so much success along the way.'

Lando Norris is also quick to acknowledge a debt to Hamilton in terms of watching and analysing his driving – and learning from it. He said Lewis had 'definitely' set the standard on the track and it was one he was keen to learn and benefit from. 'When I started watching F1, I was supporting Lewis Hamilton. Lewis was the guy at McLaren, and he was kind of a reason why I got into F1 in the first place.

'He's pretty good! Seven World Championships, over 100 wins – if I get anywhere close to that in my racing career, then I'll be pretty happy!

'When I look at Federer, Nadal and Djokovic, all basically achieved exactly the same achievements, yet have three totally different ways of playing. I'm sure they trained differently. When you see them on court, they excel on different courts [surfaces]. What I take away from that, and also from what I take away from Lewis, is that there is no one path to success.'

Hamilton himself has pointedly remarked that he knows what makes his car tick – and gets annoyed if his team ignores him completely. In 2023, for example, he said they did not listen to him while developing their car for the season.

He said they were on the wrong track before finishing fifth in the campaign's Bahrain Grand Prix opener. 'Last year, there were things I told them. I said the issues that are with the car,' he told BBC Radio 5 Live's *Chequered Flag* podcast. 'I've driven so many cars in my life, so I know what a car needs. I know what a car doesn't need. I think it's really about accountability. It's about owning up and saying, "Yeah, you know what? We didn't listen to you. It's not where it needs to be and we've got to work. We've got to look into the balance through the corners, look at all the weak points, and just huddle up as a team." That's what we do.'

Even at Ferrari, within weeks it's claimed he had racetrack disputes with their engineers over how the car should be handled. During the Miami feature race, Hamilton felt stalled by Ferrari's hesitation to swap positions with Charles Leclerc. He had the faster medium tyres and made his feelings clear on the radio: 'Have a tea break while you're at it, come on!' – clearly letting them know he wanted a quick decision . . . in his favour.

After the race, Hamilton told reporters the comments were in frustration at Ferrari's indecision. 'It wasn't even anger,' he said. 'It wasn't like, effing and blinding and anything like that. It's like, "Make a decision! You're sitting there on the chair, you've got the stuff in front of you, make the decision, quick." That's how I was. I was me; we're in a panic; we're trying to keep the car on the track. We're computing things fast.

'I've still got my fire in my belly. I could feel a bit of it really coming up there. I'm not going to apologise for being a fighter. I'm not going to apologise for still wanting it. I know everyone in the team does too. And I truly believe that when we fix some of the problems that we have with the car, we'll be back in the fight with the Mercedes, with the Red Bulls.'

He denied he had problems with Ferrari race engineer Riccardo Adami, saying they had a great relationship. After a seeming disagreement in Monaco in 2025, Hamilton laughed off claims of a fallout. He said after the race, 'It was literally just there were areas where we had radio problems through the race, and I did not get information that I wanted. We spoke afterwards. There is a lot of speculation and most of it is BS. We have a great relationship.

'He is amazing to work with. He is a great guy, working so hard, we both are. We don't always get it right every weekend. Do we have disagreements? Yes, like everyone does in relationships. But we work through them. We are both in it together.'

Lewis added, 'We both want to win a World Championship together and we are both working towards lifting the team up. So, it is just all noise and we are not paying attention to it. It doesn't make a difference to the job we are trying to do.' Hamilton said he and Adami, who previously worked with four-time world champion Sebastian Vettel and Spaniard Carlos Sainz, were learning more and more about each other and adapting the way they worked. 'He has worked with lots of different drivers before. We don't have any problems whatsoever.'

So, having put that negativity to bed, let's move on to some positivity: just what is the secret to Hamilton's success? What are the backbones of his technique, his style; what has propelled him to those seven titles and F1 immortality? Obviously, different F1 pundits and fans will have different views: these are just some observations.

One obvious aspect is Lewis's wonderful control and intuition on braking.

F1 expert Mark Hughes summed it up brilliantly on the Formulaone.com site, saying, 'Hamilton's raw speed is no greater now than when it first caused such a sensation in his 2007 rookie season . . . he's super-hard on the brakes (where the downforce generated by an F1 car means there is a lot of lap time to be had), but has a fantastic ability to match how quickly the downforce is bleeding off with his modulation of the pedal pressure so that there's no wasted grip but no locked wheels either. This is arguably the trickiest skill of all to perfect in a high-downforce car.'

Lewis is also a wizard at 'nursing' his tyres through a race: knowing how to keep them in the best condition on different sections of the track, so he gets the very best out of them. As one fan said, while calling Lewis the GOAT (Greatest of All Time), 'Tyre management is all about slowing in critical parts of the track and pushing for the rest of the lap to keep tyre temps ideal.'

Hamilton, with those championship crowns and all those years of experience, is the master of control, not just his tyres, but all parts of his car. Of course, it helps that he remains cool under all circumstances and doesn't panic. It's as if he has an inbuilt engineering computer chip in his brain. He knows instinctively when to block and when to pass, what the percentages are and whether it is doable.

In 2007, I asked Formula 1 expert Darren Simpson to provide a rundown and analysis on just this subject matter: how Hamilton has always seemed to have a natural instinct, a winner's instinct. Simpson told me Lewis was already shaping up to rival the man who, at the time, was the greatest – Michael Schumacher.

And he saw similarities on and off the track in their stylistic approach and racing techniques. Lewis had already said his aim was to emulate Schuey by winning multiple titles – and even to surpass him, although at the time that was only a pipe dream. He also made it clear he admired Michael's total commitment to claim victory and to utilising every inch of the track and the car's performance capabilities to achieve that.

Simpson's views are still valid today as we attempt to pinpoint a lineage link in the track techniques of modern-day Hamilton, Norris and Russell.

He told me that Lewis had a special quality, even back then as a rookie, that Schuey didn't. 'Lewis may match Schuey's skills, but has something the German did not possess: an ability to fight in a less aggressive way and still win the day. Schumacher resorted to daring tactics that often led to collisions. His impregnable self-belief made it impossible for him to contemplate defeat, thus legitimising in his mind the use of any conceivable tactic. And by thus intimidating opponents, he spread fear.'

There is something of the modern-day Max Verstappen in that assessment: the win-at-all-costs danger that earned him the moniker 'Mad Max' in the pits.

Simpson continued, 'Hamilton can keep his enemies at bay without them going into the barriers. He has already displayed aggression. Whether Hamilton would buckle in the face of Schumacher's invincibility is, alas, unlikely to ever be put to the test in the cauldron of Formula 1 Championship racing, but he would nonetheless relish the challenge.

'When asked which driver from the past he would most like to face, Hamilton replied: "The likes of Juan Manuel

Fangio, Alain Prost, Ayrton Senna and Michael Schumacher because I have always wanted to race against him."

'He then joked, "The year I get here, he [Michael] bales out – I don't know if I had something to do with that!" In the unpredictable world of Formula 1, where hype can make or break a driver's career (just ask Jenson Button), Lewis Hamilton is already a truly great driver.

'It is true that those who go on to achieve a higher level of success announce their arrival with verve rather than a slow build-up. Cast your mind back to Schumacher's first year, qualifying seventh on the grid in Spa on his debut, and generally showing his legendary teammate Nelson Piquet that there was a new kid on the block and he was not willing to sit patiently and wait for his turn.

'The late, great Ayrton Senna and four-time world champion Alain Prost also destroyed the competition in their first season before moving on to destroy each other. Hamilton has joined that elite group. He is calm, consistent and hard-working but also has an edge about him – for example, the way he chooses to drive so close to the wall, allowing him to maintain incredible speed coming out of corners. And the kind of tactics that he used in the US Grand Prix in 2007 against his teammate Alonso when he used a centre-to-right and then slight right-back to centre defensive overtaking manoeuvre that just about avoided punishment.

'Schumacher, however, was far more precise and rehearsed, using the stealth of a ninja. His machine-like qualities were developed on the track over many years; whereas Hamilton had been carefully crafted and tuned from an early age by one man – Ron Dennis – to be a monster the minute he hit the circuit in a tried-and-tested car.

'Comparing the two is difficult because Schumacher started in the days when cars were much less computerised with no active suspension and no traction control by way of example, whereas Hamilton started at a time when cars are almost radio-controlled. This, however, does not detract from his courage, or the natural aggression that all champions are made of.

'But there is an inescapable fact: Hamilton drives like a karter. He loves the edge of the track and takes a late turn into the hairpin and clips a late apex. In fact, his driving does reflect that of Schuey's early in the German's career.

'Lots of sharp turn-ins, lots of brake lock-ups . . . Driving so close to the wall is a breathtaking tactic while it pays off, but will he, one day, end up in the wall like Senna? Of course, we pray not . . .

'Only once was the wall a problem for Schumacher, when he broke his leg in 1999 at Silverstone. The rest of the time, Schumacher's ruthless "win at any cost" mentality, which on occasions resulted in Formula 1 driving becoming a contact sport, was the problem. Ask Damon Hill.

'One person I spoke to recently suggested that Lewis, because of his brilliance, is already in danger of becoming boring. He said: "The problem is he may be so successful with metronomic consistency that he may decide never to display the genius driving talents he may already have, or that he may develop in the future. If he wasn't English, we'd be saying he's boring like Sampras."

'Well, if metronomy wins races, then what's the problem? It is a very effective way of winning, especially if all around are being anything but metronomic and throwing their cars off the track. Both men are geniuses on the track, but in different ways when it comes to driving technique and style.'

Hamilton himself has never acknowledged being specifically influenced by British drivers of former eras in terms of racecraft. He has said how he admired the nobility and sportsmanship of Sir Stirling Moss. Hamilton often spoke of Moss not in terms of braking points or cornering lines, but of his gentlemanly spirit, his honesty and the love of competition that transcended eras. 'Two people from massively different times and backgrounds but we clicked,' Hamilton said after Moss's passing, 'and ultimately found that the love for racing we both shared made us comrades.' In Moss, Hamilton saw a model of how to carry success with dignity.

Lewis's major influence on the track, and the man he has always idolised, was Ayrton Senna. Hamilton has never hidden just how much Senna shaped the way he drives. He has said that the Brazilian legend was the blueprint he tried to copy when he began competing in karts. 'I watched Ayrton when I was young and thought: this is how I want to drive when I get the opportunity. I went out there and tried it on the kart track. My whole approach to racing has developed from there,' he explained.

That influence shows most clearly in his qualifying performances. Senna's single-lap brilliance became something

Hamilton tried to match, and he has often spoken about treating poles as vital.

When Hamilton matched Senna's tally of 65 pole positions in 2017, he admitted it was one of his greatest achievements. 'For me, Ayrton was the guy. He was the one I watched as a kid, the one who inspired me. To equal his record – it's the most emotional moment I've had in my career,' he said. It was important not simply because of the number, but because Hamilton had built his style around the standard Senna had set.

There was another link during that historic moment in Montreal. After the race, a gift was presented to him from Senna's family – one of Ayrton's helmets to mark the occasion. After holding it aloft in its glass box, and showing it to the crowd, an emotional Lewis said, 'I'm shaken. Speechless. I know that Ayrton was for many of you your favourite driver, and he was the same for me. He was the one who inspired me to be where I am today, so to match him and to receive this is the greatest honour, for the Senna family to send me this . . . I don't possess any of Ayrton's real artefacts; this is the most special thing I have, above and beyond all my trophies.

'I equalled Ayrton in race wins a while ago so this has been my focus. Literally, as a kid I thought if I was lucky I could emulate Ayrton and I can't believe it. I remember coming home from school and putting on a videotape of Ayrton, so it's really strange to think that now I'm here and I have that many poles. Ayrton was the guy who I knew at the beginning; it was the colour of the helmet, that's what you notice as a kid. And being that this is the most difficult season of my career racing great guys, and having us so close, it pushes us all to the limit; it relies on us to be perfect. Of course we can't always be perfect, but today I got as close as I could get. I am honoured to be honoured by that family and honestly I couldn't be happier. To Ayrton and his family, God bless you, thank you.'

Lewis hit gold on his second lap in qualifying, equalling Senna's lap record with 1m 11.459s. He told reporters it was 'a sexy lap!'. Then added, 'A great lap. I can't believe it came together so well. You can only hope and imagine that it's going to go well and sometimes it doesn't, but the lap started beautifully, and I just built it, smoothly, no mistakes.

'The first section was fantastic, and I just managed to build up a bit more in each one, and the team did such a great job to make up for the mistakes in the last race.'

Sebastian Vettel was second in 1m 11.789s and was generous in acknowledging Hamilton's historic feat. 'Equalling Ayrton is a massive achievement, and Lewis was the better man today. I wasn't entirely happy at the start of qualifying, but it got better and better and I was able to step it up for the last run. But I lost the car a bit in Turn 2 and was on the back foot already, and knew I had to catch up, but he had enough. I would have loved to have had a better lap at the end, but that's the way it is.'

The link with Senna is also clear in Hamilton's skills in changeable or wet conditions, where the Brazilian was also legendary. In races like Silverstone 2008 or Istanbul 2020, Hamilton showed the same talent for finding grip and improvising as conditions changed. 'It's about feeling where the grip is, being brave enough to go looking for it, even when no one else does,' he explained – words that could just as easily have come from the legendary Brazilian driver.

Of course, Istanbul in November 2020 was no ordinary race. It was the moment when Hamilton equalled Schumacher's seven titles as he roared to victory in the Turkish GP in tough conditions. Starting sixth on the grid, he showed his total mastery in the rain by romping home in what was also his 94th career GP triumph. Afterwards, he was in tears and initially lost for words. Finally, he said, 'I've got to say thank you to my family. We dreamed of this when we were young, watching the Grand Prix, and this is way, way beyond our dreams. It's so important for kids – dream the impossible. You've got to work for it, chase it and never give up or doubt yourself.'

It was the culmination of all those hours of hard work over all those years, streamlining and perfecting his racing technique and dominant driving style, all towards this one impossible dream. Only he had now made the dream come true.

It would be much to live up to for any British driver following in his slipstream. Impossible, really, but in Lando Norris and George Russell, Britain now had a duo who were determined to carve out their own legend. In their own ways, and their own styles, perfecting their own techniques towards glory. But with a nod of gratitude to Hamilton for his influence.

In the case of Norris, many pundits had argued that his

Achilles heel is that he is at times too cautious – compared to his main rivals, Piastri and Verstappen. Yet in April 2024, Lando seemed to indicate that he was too aggressive; that his attacking driving style had become a concern. He suggested that the way the McLaren was now set up and the bigger tyres meant he was rethinking his approach.

He said, 'In qualifying, I've always been wanting to push quite a bit more in certain areas and kind of want to go out and just be attacking. And I have to do the complete opposite. It's a hard one to get my head around because I want to go out and find another level in qualifying, and you just can't do that with these tyres and with our car. You almost have to drive it the opposite way.

'So there's something, almost from being used to the cars a few years ago, that's kind of punishing me now and not adapting quick enough. But that's something that's up to me. That's my job to adapt and to do a better job on, but also just with how our car is, how you have to drive it, it continues to be quite a tricky car to drive. To execute a perfect qualifying lap every single time, it's not an easy thing to do. But it's something we're working on.'

He had been known to hit the brakes as late as possible on corners, but that wasn't always effective – especially in qualifying sessions. He had spent time in the McLaren simulator to process different approaches, and he said, 'It's tough, because it's not always the best correlation. There are certain techniques and abilities of trying to drive relaxed. Those are the kind of things you can do on the simulator. But recreating that exact emotion of when you're in the car, and you're going for a qualifying lap, it's not easy to replicate such a thing on a simulator.'

In the 2025 season, he actually conceded that the McLaren MCL39 wasn't ideal for the way he liked to race. He told reporters, 'I've got to a point where I've just accepted that you can't really have a car that suits your driving. I stopped maybe asking so much for exactly what I want and am more just willing to do whatever makes the car quicker. It is probably a tricky car to drive and to put together laps. But clearly, it's taken a step forward from last year.' He admitted it wasn't what he wanted to 'push the entries' and 'push the braking'.

He said, 'It has similar characteristics to the last car and some of those characteristics I don't like – and do not suit the way I want to drive in an attacking way. It doesn't suit me in terms of me wanting to push the entries and push the braking. It's very weak, I would say, from that point of view. So not what I like, but at the same time, some of it is down to the adaptation of needing to change my driving styles a little bit every year. The car I drive this year is very different to what a McLaren was a few years ago, clearly, because we were at the back and now we're at the front. But I'll just drive whatever car I have to drive as long as it's fighting for a win and quick enough to fight for a win. Then, I'm just happy to drive what I get.'

George Russell is often praised for a driving style that looks calm, measured and almost minimalist compared to some rivals. Russell tends to be smooth, precise and deliberate. He keeps the car balanced by trusting his initial inputs, rather than scrambling to fix mistakes later.

This approach also shows up in how he manages races. Russell is known for thinking a few steps ahead, saving his tyres and energy while maintaining a competitive pace. Instead of diving into every gap or making aggressive moves, he waits for the right opportunities. It can make him look less dramatic on track, but it nonetheless often pays off over a long race.

He is efficient. By doing less, Russell often achieves more.

His style allows him to stay consistent, reduce wear on the car, and keep cool in pressure situations.

In 2024, in 24 qualifying sessions, he outperformed Mercedes teammate Lewis Hamilton 18 times and beat him in sprint qualifying. He said his minimalist technique had helped him achieve his results: 'I think my natural driving style probably worked well with these cars.

'But, at the same time, my record in qualifying against my previous teammates was good, and in every category, my qualifying results were solid. I don't think there's anything particular about this generation. But, obviously, Lewis has been my toughest teammate, so I think that's why it's highlighted a bit more.'

Tyre handling and staying cool when under enormous pressure were also key to George's growing reputation as one of F1's top performers and technicians. He told motorsport.com, 'You learn over the course of the season what to do to get the most out of the tyres, where you can exploit the car's strengths, and where you need to be cautious of its weaknesses.

'I know exactly where the strengths and weaknesses

are and the areas where I need to pay attention. I think I'm pretty good at turning the page and moving on [when things don't turn out as good] while learning from those moments. When I was younger, I'd most likely have dwelled on things longer. Now, even if I'm behind in an FP3 session, or even in Q2, I don't stress. I know that what happened before doesn't matter. It's that one lap in Q3 that will make the difference.'

In August 2024, therace.com illustrated the driving styles, at the time, of Norris – in comparison with Hamilton – in this way, 'When The Race revisited every single qualifying performance so far, reviewed onboard footage and compared telemetry between Hamilton and Russell, two distinctly different approaches from the two drivers became apparent. Russell brakes fractionally earlier, but starts turning much later, and carries more speed through the corner and exiting it. Whereas Hamilton brakes later but starts turning in earlier.'

In conclusion for this chapter, Hamilton accelerated Russell's development. Norris, while more indirect, acknowledges that Hamilton was an inspiration for his entry into, and passion for, Formula 1.

Both grew up watching Hamilton drive – so it's inevitable that, in different ways, they would be influenced by him. Both witnessed him at his majestic peak, and as young British drivers coming through the ranks, he was the example they measured themselves against.

Hamilton's style has always been a blend of smoothness and aggression – knowing when to be patient and when to strike – and there are echoes of that in how Russell and Norris handle themselves.

Russell has a similar smooth, economical approach. He doesn't fight the car. He tries to keep things tidy, making a move when his instincts tell him – and trusting them. That calmness under pressure, of not over-driving, feels like a direct influence from Hamilton's years of winning races without burning through his tyres.

Norris, meanwhile, has picked up on Hamilton's balance between speed and racecraft. He's daring when he needs to be, but also thinks about a race in long-game terms – rather than just the next corner.

Neither of them are copies – they've each shaped their own style – but Hamilton gave them a model of how a modern Formula 1 car should be driven. In different ways, they've taken parts of his approach and built it into something new, carrying that influence with them every time they get into their cars.

CHAPTER 9

THE 'FACTORY'

It's a neat coincidence for this book's analysis that Lewis Hamilton and Lando Norris gained their differing 'apprenticeships' in the same 'club' – or as some have dubbed it, the same 'Formula 1 Factory'. Both were trained up by McLaren although it was Lewis who would receive the full membership benefit. He joined McLaren's development programme at a very young age (after impressing Ron Dennis at that karting awards dinner in 1998). McLaren and Mercedes backed him financially through the junior categories all the way to Formula 1, where he debuted with McLaren in 2007.

As for Lando, the *Guardian* newspaper in 2018 confidently stated that, 'Still only 18, Norris is part of the McLaren young driver programme and is in demand.' They were correct in saying he was 'in demand', but unlike Hamilton, his McLaren entry was more of a fast-track internship at

17, while Lewis was a full scholarship apprentice, from the age of 13.

Lewis was a fully 'home-grown' McLaren driver while Lando was recruited later in life as a rising talent.

Lando joined as a junior/reserve driver after winning the McLaren Autosport BRDC Award. From there, he became their test and reserve driver before being promoted to a full race seat in 2019.

Given the rigours and daily demands of the programme, as described by Hamilton, Norris was perhaps fortunate to miss out on the tough and taxing scheme! The way Lewis portrayed it over the years, it was the hardest of apprenticeships, one that demanded total commitment and, in many ways, was a tale of lost youth. There were few opportunities to go out with pals at the weekend, or to relax listening to music. Total commitment was the name of the game as McLaren were financing a programme to make the chosen few potential world champions in Formula 1.

As we will see below, while Hamilton repaid them seven times over, another duo found it impossible to deliver similar success.

In Lando's case, as a late recruit, he would learn swiftly and by 2025 seemed on course to follow in Hamilton's footsteps, potentially becoming world champion as he fought with teammate Oscar Piastri for the Drivers' Championship crown.

Hamilton would tell of the intense nature of the McLaren training programme as he progressed in F1. How the days were long and hard, full of testing, practice and other rigours. It would involve much time spent in the McLaren Technology Centre at Woking, Surrey.

Commenting in 2007 as the countdown to his F1 debut continued, Lewis said, 'I am in the McLaren Technology Centre every day. I have relocated to Woking to be close to the team and the facility. I train every day in the gym, meet team members for training and development sessions, and generally get to know the team and watch closely the progress of the new car. It also gives me the chance to work closely with my new engineers and for us to get to know each other like the back of our hands!'

Ron Dennis was unhappy when certain pundits suggested that he had created Hamilton via the Tech Centre; that Lewis was merely a factory-manufactured Formula 1 driver: 'First of all, we've done it for several young karters. We constructed a karting team for both Lewis and Nico Rosberg. Obviously, they've both done a great job and Nico – though really more because of his age than anything and the way the licensing system works – I think he just stepped ahead as regards getting into Formula 1 a little earlier.

'But I was always keen for Lewis to dominate every category in which he raced because that gives you a certain mindset and we wanted him to follow the right path into Formula 1. But it's important to remember, no matter who gives an opportunity to young drivers, ultimately it's their own abilities, their commitment, their own dedication and sacrifices, that determines the result. I will never, ever claim to be the reason that Lewis is the great success he is.

'That is his own effort and his own commitment. Yes, he's

had an opportunity; yes, he hasn't had to worry about money, but the most difficult thing is actually to deliver, given those opportunities, and that's all down to him and obviously the support of his family.'

The training was heavy going, though. Most days Lewis was left exhausted but also exhilarated. He quickly realised that it would give him a head start in the race to not only get to F1, but hopefully to dominate it, too.

The *Sunday Times* described the demanding sessions as 'astonishing in their intensity'. The newspaper added: 'High-tech telemetric read-outs enable the driver and engineers to refine lap times down by fractions of a second, while racing simulators and 3-D virtual reality cars mean drivers can know a circuit off by heart without having driven it for real.

'Some reports have claimed Hamilton has spent thousands of hours in such a simulator at the McLaren base in Woking, although Hamilton downplays its influence.'

He had indeed spent hours in the simulator, and in the gym, and was busy building up his strength and resilience in readiness for the big time.

The *Daily Telegraph* highlighted just how strong the boy was becoming in a magazine feature: 'He is 5ft 10in, 10st 10lb and has a 16.5in neck, broad shoulders and a superbly developed upper body. His forearms are streaked with pulsating veins like brown thunderbolts . . .

'For six months before the start of the season, Hamilton was groomed for his Formula 1 debut. Every day, including weekends, he submitted himself to two three-hour training sessions: he swam 2 kilometres, cycled 50 miles and spent two hours in the gym. "It's all about endurance," he says. "There is nothing worse than getting to mid-race and starting to fatigue, because your mind needs to work doubly hard to give energy to the rest of your body, and then you lose focus and you can crash. It is about your mind being at ease that you are fit enough."'

The respected motorsport journalist Richard Williams possibly risked the ire of Ron Dennis as he mentioned the word 'robotic' in a portrait for the *Guardian* of Lewis's training. He noted Hamilton had been brought through in a 'training period that included thousands of hours in the McLaren team's unique and highly secret simulator' and 'some of the specific training techniques brought to bear on astronauts and fighter pilots'.

He provided the most in-depth illustration of just what Hamilton had experienced at McLaren. Williams went on, '[Ron] Dennis put at Hamilton's disposal the greatest learning tool that any driver has ever been given. McLaren's simulator, developed over the past eight years at a cost estimated to be above £20 million, has been Hamilton's schoolroom, where he sits in a full-size Formula 1 car, minus wheels and a functioning engine, in a darkened room in front of a large, curved plasma screen.

'The chassis is suspended on a multi-point hydraulic rig that moves in response to his touches on the steering wheel and pedals as he watches a circuit unfold on the screen, with appropriate sound effects.'

It sounded almost like something out of a James Bond 007 movie. 'Everything in this grown-up video game is programmed via the simulator's software: the minutest details of the circuit, the response of the engine under different conditions, the type and wear-rate of the tyres, as well as the noise of the engine.'

Lewis had undergone a nine-year training period, the likes of which no other Formula 1 driver had ever done before.

So, yes, he was, in that sense, the prototype of the new breed of driver; developed from an early age to be a champion.

He himself admitted before the British Grand Prix in 2007 that the £5 million training programme had elevated him to a position that few could expect to match. 'I don't think you get to this position without working hard, as they've said. I was given an opportunity. I remember Ron said, "You have the opportunity, but I want you to be the fittest guy out there," and so I had to make sure, even in my own self-confidence and self-belief, I wanted to be the fittest out there. Whether I am or not, who knows?

'I had an opportunity to have a training programme, [to] learn as much as I could about the car, so that I got to the first race and I had no problems. And we didn't look back and say, "I wish we had done this differently," or, "I wish we had worked an extra day." We took every day as it came and really maximised every day. This is what I've been working for so many years, so when you get the opportunity, you don't just let it pass by, you get as much out of it as you can.'

The programme had also drilled into him the idea that knowing as much about the workings of the car could be just as important as the driving of it.

It was a dual requirement to be the best. So he continually took in software and mechanical knowledge via data, books and videos. His head would sometimes spin, such was the amount of information to digest.

'I have had my head buried in books for the past nine months. When I'm not looking at books, I am watching DVDs or talking to the McLaren team about the car. The cars have so much software these days – it's not just mechanical. You don't just get into a car and drive it around a track; you have to learn about aerodynamics.

'I've been studying from September to March to make sure that I have it in my head. Then I have to study each individual track. The advice I would give to other drivers is never to give up, even if you spin off. I think once I spun off and I got back on and focused and ended up coming second.'

'You just can't afford to lose focus. When I am driving at 200mph, if I lose focus then I could die, so it kind of puts it into perspective.'

Fellow Brit David Coulthard had also massively benefited from McLaren training after joining the team in 1996 as a fully-fledged race driver. By then, he was already a proven F1 racer, so McLaren did not develop him as part of their young driver programme. But they gave him access to the simulator, fitness programme and technical training. He later conceded that it had all been helpful in his career.

At a press conference before the British Grand Prix in July 2007, he told how his experiences there suggested to him that Lewis Hamilton, with a full-on McLaren programme over many years, would be hard to beat on the track.

He explained, 'Having been part of the McLaren system, I know some of the facilities that they had up to the point that I left, and I would be surprised if any Grand Prix team has quite as complete a package in simulation devices that the drivers can use. It's obviously a state-of-the-art facility, more modern probably than anyone else's out there.

'But Lewis has had to prove himself, otherwise he wouldn't be sitting here. It's not charity work that McLaren are doing. They invested because they saw the talent and they've helped him develop that over the time. As Lewis inevitably moves offshore and grows into his life, he will inevitably spend less time at the factory because there just won't be the time. He will need energy, recovery time to maintain the level that he's achieved already over the next ten to 15 years.'

The idea that Lewis was Ron Dennis's F1 creation found credence when it emerged that Ron had hired Dr Kerry Spackman, a New Zealand-born neuroscientist, apparently to turn the boy into a race-winning machine. Spackman's research had shown that while in Formula 1 some cars are faster than others, it was ultimately the driver who is the key to better speed.

Robert Matthews in the online news magazine, thefirstpost.co.uk, spoke of Spackman's scientific 'engineering'. 'A major part of Spackman's approach is the intensive use of computer simulators, which expose Hamilton to every twist, turn and eventuality of a race until dealing with them is utterly instinctive.'

'It was the same approach NASA had to astronaut training more than 40 years previously. Spackman, however, goes much further, applying insights from neuroscience and psychology to create a more comprehensive picture of Hamilton's technique and mindset, and bring his foibles under control.

'The result is a driver who combines the standard skillset of focus and controlled aggression with relentless consistency.'

Kevin Magnussen and Stoffel Vandoorne also benefited from McLaren's young driver system. Both were hand-picked as prospects who could make an impact in F1. Magnussen's link with McLaren began in 2010 when the team signed him up as one of its rising stars. Coming from a racing family – his father Jan Magnussen had been in Formula 1 briefly in the 1990s – Kevin had the potential and the pedigree. McLaren backed him with resources, helping to map out his progress through the junior ranks. The highlight came in 2013 when he won the Formula Renault 3.5 Championship, a series that at the time was seen as a legitimate stepping stone to Formula 1.

That triumph confirmed McLaren's investment had been well placed, and the team rewarded him with a race seat for the 2014 season. On his debut in Melbourne, he finished on the podium, a moment that suggested a star might be about to shine. Yet it didn't work out that way. Despite his raw speed, Magnussen's future became uncertain as McLaren juggled its line-up, leaving him on the fringes after just one full season.

McLaren's own website explained his situation in this way in 2023: 'Kevin's 2013 season concluded with him being awarded the Formula 1 drive, racing alongside Jenson Button for 2014. If that added pressure, Kev quickly shrugged it aside with his trademark mixture of smiling charm and wilful insouciance.

'Kevin enjoyed a dream debut at the Australian Grand Prix, running at the front for the whole weekend. His third-place finish on the road became second following the disqualification of Daniel Ricciardo's Red Bull. Kevin's was the best result for an F1 debutant since Jacques Villeneuve also finished second at the same track back in 1996.

'If the rest of the '14 season didn't quite live up to the lofty expectations established in that series opener, Kevin still drove with all the passion and bravery that would go on to typify his F1 career and racked up an impressive 55 points in the championship in the process.

'Through no fault of his own, Kev wasn't retained for the following season, although he made a one-off appearance in Australia as a super-sub for the injured Fernando Alonso. With drives at Renault and Haas under his belt since departing McLaren, Kevin has turned into a fine, combative and much-admired racer who has earned support and respect from many within the F1 community.'

Vandoorne's trajectory was similarly far from being a stellar one. Neither he nor Magnussen would hit anywhere near the heights of Hamilton, Norris or Coulthard.

Signed by McLaren in 2013, Vandoorne impressed with both speed and composure. He won the Formula Renault Eurocup in 2012 and was runner-up to Magnussen in the 2013 Formula Renault 3.5 Series.

Where Magnussen could be fiery and aggressive, Vandoorne was often praised for his intelligence and coolness under pressure. McLaren placed him in Formula Renault 3.5, then GP2, and his rise was impressive. By 2015, he had conquered GP2 with a campaign widely regarded as one of the most dominant the series had witnessed. His reward was the role of reserve driver at McLaren, a frustrating position for an ambitious guy.

For years he waited in the wings, testing, learning and preparing for his big chance.

When Fernando Alonso was injured in 2016, it seemed his moment had arrived, and Vandoorne stepped in and scored points on his debut in Bahrain. But the joy didn't last, as the McLaren website pointed out in 2023: 'Stoffel made his Formula 1 debut, deputising for Fernando Alonso in the 2016 Bahrain Grand Prix. It was a last-minute call-up, which involved him flying overnight from a Super Formula test session in Japan to arrive at the Bahrain circuit hours ahead of the first Formula 1 practice session.

'Despite his inexperience – he had never driven the MP4-31 before the race weekend – he performed flawlessly, out-qualifying teammate Jenson Button, and scoring the team's first World Championship point of the campaign.

'Stoffel graduated to a full-time race seat in 2017, working hard to compensate for the car's deficiencies during a difficult maiden Grand Prix season. It was a tough year, marked by multiple grid penalties for power unit changes, but seventh places in Singapore and Malaysia showed promise.

'Hopes were high for 2018, but again the team endured

a difficult season. Stoffel earned points in three of the four opening races, but thereafter he was dogged by bad luck, and he struggled to get the results that he truly deserved. He has made a fresh start by moving to Formula E, where he currently drives for Mercedes.'

For George Russell, there would be no McLaren Young Driver Scheme, but he would benefit in his late teens from support provided by the MercedesAMG Petronas Junior Team. It was a similar deal to Lando's at McLaren for the 19-year-old. Russell impressed Mercedes with his performances in European Formula 3 and, in late 2016, reached out to team principal, Toto Wolff, seeking support. In his usual meticulous approach to life, George crafted a detailed PowerPoint about why he deserved a spot in their junior programme.

Wolff invited him in as a simulator driver and eventually offered to back his racing programme. Russell officially joined Mercedes' junior ranks at the beginning of 2017, becoming one of only three members of the programme at that time, alongside Pascal Wehrlein and Esteban Ocon.

That support wasn't just financial. It meant access to resources, testing and the kind of guidance that helps a young driver focus fully on racing. Reflecting on what being a rookie within such a giant of motorsport meant, Russell said, 'It is great to be a part of the Junior Programme . . . It is an incredible opportunity to have the backing of the Formula 1 world champions . . . I am working with people who are the best in the business, who I know will help me develop as a driver and as a person.'

George didn't waste the opportunity. He won the GP3 title in his first season under Mercedes, then followed it up with the Formula 2 Championship a year later, proving himself against the best of his generation. Those results made him impossible to ignore, and when the time came to step into Formula 1, Mercedes placed him at Williams, one of their engine customers, for the 2019 season. It was a tough introduction, given Williams's struggles at the time, but he did well, all considered.

The path Mercedes set him on eventually led back to them, with Russell becoming a full-time Mercedes driver and race winner. In the same way McLaren's programme paved the way for Hamilton and Norris, the Mercedes junior scheme played a decisive role in Russell's rise, turning him from a promising late teen hopeful into one of the leading names on the grid.

In 2025, Mercedes announced an expanded junior roster and George was asked to comment on the impact the scheme had had on his development. He said, 'The Junior Programme has been such a big part of my life. I think the one thing I'm most grateful for is the support that everyone in the team gave me to help me perform. They didn't just drop me in situations and pile on the pressure.

'For all 12 of the current junior drivers, I know they will have the very best support and structure to help them on their motorsport journey.

'With Kimi [Antonelli] and I, both Junior Programme graduates, racing in F1 for the team this year, it shows what is possible. I am sure every one of the juniors will be giving it their all this year and I look forward to seeing their success on track.'

Fellow junior graduate Antonelli added, 'The Junior Programme helped me develop so much, not only as a driver but also as a person. I'm so grateful . . . without it, I don't think I would be sitting here as a works Mercedes driver in F1.'

The path Mercedes set Antonelli and Russell on eventually led to them becoming full-time Mercedes drivers and, in George's case, an F1 race winner. In the same way McLaren's programme paved the way for Hamilton and Norris, the Mercedes junior scheme played a decisive role in Russell's rise, turning him from a promising youngster into a genuine contender for the World Championship crown.

CHAPTER 10

RIVALRY

It's 2007 and Lewis Hamilton is in his debut Formula 1 season. As a rookie at McLaren, he may have been expected to toe the line behind his teammate, Fernando Alonso, especially as the Spaniard was the reigning world champion. But his innate ambition and desire to win meant that was against his very nature – while Alonso was also fiery and fully committed. In his eyes, he was not only team number one, but world number one, so of course he should have special treatment. His sense of entitlement didn't sit well with young Lewis and the two would frequently clash over the season.

Alonso also seemed to take umbrage at the fact that Lewis received better treatment within the team, and the media, because he was British – and McLaren was based in the UK.

At the time, I asked one of the McLaren crew if this was why they seemed so behind their new boy. On condition of anonymity, they hinted at the team's thinking on the feud between Lewis and his teammate Fernando Alonso, ever present in his debut campaign.

'The thing is there's been all this stuff in the press with Alonso saying we favour Lewis because he is British . . . but that's rubbish. We're all in this together; we're all McLaren. Big Ron [Ron Dennis] wouldn't have any of that kind of thing in his team – if anything, it was Lewis as the rookie who got the slower car.

'But Lewis is a special talent – he works harder than most seasoned drivers and he's got that touch of magic that most don't have. I watch him in the practice sessions and it reminds me of why I wanted to be part of Formula 1 in the first place.

'A lot of the time it seems that Alonso's raging, that he's flat out, trying to cling on to his title, but Lewis was often beating him hands down – looking as if he hasn't broken sweat, always gracious and the crowds love him.

'The thing is, Alonso's a great driver, a great champion and nice guy underneath it all, but Lewis is something special. Forget all the stuff about being the first black guy and all that – he could be the best driver of his generation irrelevant of all that. It gives me the shivers to be around that, to see it happening, and, yes, even Big Ron's got a spring in his step these days.'

Of course, the duo were far from being the only ones to not see things eye to eye in the ultra-competitive world of F1.

The paddock has always been awash with gossip of various fallouts between teammates over the following two decades, as indeed it had been since the very start of the sport. Currently, George Russell is regularly involved in spats on and off the track with Max Verstappen and had a run-in with teammate Alex Albon while both raced for Williams.

Meanwhile, Norris initially appeared at odds with teammate Carlos Sainz, when Lando first raced in F1, and now battles competitively with Oscar Piastri – although in both instances no rancour survived or survives now after racing is completed. It's not really in Lando's nature to hold grudges, and he even remains friends with Verstappen, despite the Dutchman sporadically cutting him up on the track. We'll examine these cases later in this chapter, but first it's back to Hamilton and pre-Hamilton to give the issue a broader feel.

Few rivalries in sport – let alone Formula 1 – have matched the intensity, drama and sheer magnetism of Ayrton Senna versus Alain Prost. Spanning from 1988 to 1993, their clashes were not simply about race wins or championships; they were philosophical battles fought on the tarmac, in the media and behind closed garage doors.

Senna, the Brazilian maestro, drove with unyielding aggression and a near-mystical belief in his destiny.

Prost, the Frenchman known as 'The Professor', relied on meticulous preparation, political acumen and clinical precision. Their contrasting styles made them natural adversaries. When McLaren paired them as teammates in 1988, it was always going to be the most combustible of mixes.

That first season set the tone. McLaren's dominance was absolute – the team won 15 of 16 races – but Senna emerged as champion, unsettling Prost. For the Frenchman, it was a reminder that raw speed could overpower calculation. For Senna, it was confirmation of his belief that talent and courage should reign supreme.

By 1989, the relationship had soured beyond repair.

At the Japanese Grand Prix in Suzuka, Prost led the championship. When Senna attempted a daring pass at the chicane, the two collided. Prost retired immediately, but Senna rejoined, won the race and was then disqualified for a supposed rules breach. The title went to Prost, and the political undercurrents were laid bare.

The animosity deepened after Prost departed for Ferrari in 1990, and fate brought them together again in Japan. This time, Senna was in control of the championship. Angered that pole position had been placed on the 'dirty' side of the grid, he vowed to retaliate if Prost got ahead. True to his word, Senna rammed Prost at the first corner, securing the title in one of the most controversial acts in Formula 1 history.

Later, Senna admitted the move was deliberate, justifying it as redress for perceived injustices.

Despite their hostility, there were moments of begrudging respect. They pushed each other to the limits of their abilities, creating races that would go down in F1 legend. In 1993, when Prost returned from a year-long sabbatical to drive for Williams, he again had the upper hand, winning his fourth championship. Senna, still at McLaren, fought valiantly with an inferior car, but the gap was insurmountable.

Prost retired at the end of 1993, and in one of the most

unexpected gestures in sport, Senna invited him to join him on the podium in Adelaide and publicly acknowledged his old rival.

It was a fleeting glimpse of the mutual admiration that lay buried beneath years of bitterness. Tragically, less than a year later, Senna would die at Imola, leaving Prost to reflect openly on how much the Brazilian had meant to him.

The Senna–Prost rivalry remains a benchmark for competitive intensity. It was not merely a contest of speed but of ideology: instinct versus intellect, raw courage versus calculated precision. Each man's greatness was, in many ways, forged by the other, and their battles left an indelible mark on Formula 1's history – a reminder that the sport's fiercest rivalries often create its finest moments.

Yet there would be no such nobleness in Lewis Hamilton's feud with Fernando Alonso. That 2007 season would witness a multitude of run-ins, fallouts, accusations and resentment as the seasoned pro battled to put the young whipper-snapper firmly in his place. Alonso came into McLaren as the reigning double world champion (2005 and 2006 with Renault) and believed Hamilton, the rookie, would support his own title bid.

But Hamilton matched Alonso's pace from the first race – finishing third to Alonso's runner-up in Australia – and then went on a run of nine consecutive podiums. By mid-season, Hamilton was leading the championship and made clear his view of how the season was panning out, 'I don't see myself as anyone's number two. I'm here to race.'

That certainly clashed with Alonso's ego. He argued that

team orders or preferential strategy should be due to him as the senior driver.

Events at the Monaco GP that year solidified the sense that the duo were at loggerheads, and that both were unhappy with how the team were handling them. Hamilton finished runner-up behind Alonso but felt the team had prevented him from challenging for the win. Afterwards, he said, 'I was told to slow down. I think the team had their own agenda.'

Meanwhile, Alonso made his own view clear, saying that Hamilton needed to 'understand how the team works'.

There was a further flashpoint in qualifying in Hungary. Alonso delayed leaving the pits, preventing Hamilton from getting in his final timed lap. The FIA penalised Alonso by demoting him five grid places. But many fans and pundits viewed the incident as another example of Alonso's frustration with Hamilton, in this instance because the younger driver had earlier refused to follow team instructions to give Alonso track position. Team boss Ron Dennis openly admitted his ire at Alonso's intransigence, saying, 'I'm not going to comment on why Fernando sat there . . . we are unhappy with the situation.'

The incident caused a temporary rift between Dennis and the young man he had trained for nine years to become a champion. In a heated post-qualifying exchange, Dennis ended up throwing his headphones at the pit wall. Most pundits believed this was over his anger at Alonso impeding Lewis in the pit lane but subsequent analysis of the radio traffic between Dennis and his protégé came up with a different reason.

Lewis, angered by the delay, had blamed it on Dennis, allegedly screaming over the team radio: 'Don't ever f****** do that to me again!' Dennis reportedly hit back, blasting: 'Don't ever f****** speak to me like that!' Lewis is said to have responded: 'Go f****** swivel!' Dennis later denied the conversations had taken place.

Some pundits argued that Dennis was too often taking Alonso's side precisely because he was Spanish and world champion – to show he wasn't overbiased towards his British protégé. He had always claimed parity between his two drivers.

For 25 years, Ron Dennis had run a team based on parity. Now he had signed a double world champion on break-the-bank wages. If you'd splashed out all that cash on the world champion, you'd probably be happy if he won again and Lewis was runner-up.

Dennis's problem appeared to stem from an unusual flaw in assessing Lewis Hamilton. He knew better than anyone that the boy was a winner, but what he hadn't imagined is that he could have been a winner in his first season – otherwise, why bring in Alonso to bring home the title in the first place?

Also, he hadn't counted on Lewis's determination to grab Alonso's crown; again, he knew his personality better than most, but even he had been surprised at Hamilton's unflinching ambition to become world champion rather than world number two.

For Alonso, the problem was of a different nature: was Lewis Hamilton the better driver, even though he was so young and a rookie? Certainly, the results suggested so. The public also seemed to agree and maybe it was that, more than anything, that riled him. Despite the outstanding achievement of being double world champion, he was not receiving the public acclaim that should accompany such an achievement.

Fernando certainly did not win the support of British fans trackside. Many viewed him as being entitled with what appeared to be constant sniping, rather than helping his teammate adapt to F1. Another couple of examples of this were highlighted just before and just after the Hungarian race. Alonso was asked to contribute to a magazine's efforts to help a charity. *F1 Racing* asked all 22 current Formula 1 drivers to sketch a picture of their teammate. Lewis's doodle was a nondescript, but pleasant image of Alonso, while Fernando's work was much more dismissive. He drew Lewis in his McLaren leathers and on the right-hand collar he had written the word 'McLaren' and on the left the word 'Boy'.

The magazine's executives couldn't hide their surprise. In an accompanying caption, they wrote: 'Notice the word "Boy" scrawled by Alonso on Lewis's shoulder . . .'

Alonso finished a credible fourth in the actual race but seemed peeved that Lewis had won. Asked if he would be at McLaren in three years' time, he said, enigmatically, 'I don't know.' Kevin Garside of the *Daily Telegraph* summed up Alonso's comments in this way: 'Cleverly he has allowed questions about his future to hang in the air. If McLaren team principal Ron Dennis believes there is a real danger of the champion slipping through his fingers with two years of a contract still to run, might he not be minded to meet Alonso's demands from the team over the course of a tight run-in?'

And Fernando refused to let it go, again commenting on the qualifying track position dispute. He told reporters, 'What happened was something new for the team. Hamilton not listening, disobeying them, was something they hadn't experienced and I guess they wanted to make him see that. But anyway, in the next race I guess everything will be back to normal and we will both try to win the race.'

On the other hand, and in the interest of fairness, Alonso did deserve some of our sympathy. He had been drafted in to win the title for a British team . . . but suddenly it was a British team with a new boy who was not only British, but British and brilliant. Also, Alonso himself was racing under an emotional dark cloud for much of the season when he learned one of his closest friends, Emmanuel Longobardi, had been killed in a helicopter accident.

He admitted it had left him 'a little bit frozen'.

During that debut season, Hamilton was asked if he was surprised by Alonso's jibes about favouritism. He said: 'I find it strange because I feel that ever since he joined the team, the team have been extremely motivated to push us both towards winning. Ron and the other guys on the team have been working very hard to make sure we have equal opportunity. It's probably always going to be difficult in a business, but obviously I've got a great relationship with all the guys in the team because I've been with them since I was 13.

'At the end of the day when Fernando came into the team,

they were extremely excited and, I feel, built a very good relationship with him. So I don't see why he would say that. But I guess because he is Spanish and I am English, he might feel that way, but I don't agree with it personally.'

But he did agree that Alonso had likely been surprised by his own race results. Lewis said, 'I doubt very much that he was expecting me to do as well as I have. But I don't know whether that's why he would be saying what he's saying. But definitely coming into the team he's the two-time world champion and he's not really been challenged – well, I think he has [had] some challenges in the past but not really had probably someone as close as me. So it's a very difficult situation.'

Alonso, when asked the same question, admitted: 'Yes, and no. I think we knew from the winter tests that Lewis was very quick and was very close times compared with Pedro [de la Rosa] and me. So, no big difference between the three drivers of the team. So, you know, why not fight for victories, podiums and Championships? But on the other hand, I think it has been a surprise for me, and a surprise for everybody, to see him doing so well and leading the championship at this point.'

The pair managed to get through to the end of the season without open warfare breaking out, but it was clear that, as the American band Sparks once sang, this town wasn't big enough for the both of them. After the bickering and antagonism, neither would walk away with the world title. No, the Iceman, Kimi Räikkönen, would lift that trophy. But Hamilton would win his personal war with Alonso, beating the double champion to runner-up spot, with the Spaniard third. It was still a quite remarkable achievement for an F1 rookie, all the more so when you consider he was only three points from winning the coveted crown. For Alonso, the outcome was probably even more disappointing as he finished on the same number of points, 109, as Lewis. But Lewis outgunned him by virtue of race success countback. Each driver had won four races, but Hamilton had five second-place finishes to Alonso's four.

And, in a sense, Lewis also won not that battle, but the war itself. For, after just one season at McLaren, Alonso exited sharply, just one year into a three-year contract, returning to Renault for the next campaign.

Moving on to George Russell and Hamilton . . . and a rivalry that was much more civilised and amiable when George arrived at Mercedes.

George became a full-time driver at the team on 7 September 2021, replacing Valtteri Bottas for the 2022 F1 season. Before that, his main connection to Mercedes was through the junior driver programme and his stand-in drive for Hamilton at the 2020 Sakhir GP after Lewis was sidelined with Covid. George showed his potential by nearly winning on debut for the team.

The Russell–Hamilton partnership at Mercedes transcended a typical teammate rivalry. Instead, it was a masterclass in respectful competition, mentorship and friendship. Russell challenged Hamilton on the track while emerging as a team player off it – a relationship defined not by simmering rivalry, but by admiration and evolution.

Russell knew from day one that he was working with the master. It was an opportunity to learn and lap up the experience on offer from the greatest driver ever in the sport. To his credit, George proved a valued apprentice, but also showed that he deserved his seat. He outscored Hamilton in two of their three seasons together, amassed three wins to Hamilton's two, and out-qualified the legend 39–29 across their shared time behind the wheel – an impressive feat for any teammate, let alone a newcomer.

But Russell was quick to acknowledge Hamilton's role in his growth. Reflecting on his first year, he said, 'From my experience, I can say that I learned more in my first year alongside Lewis than in the three years at Williams.'

It wasn't just on the track and in the paddock that George benefited from working alongside Lewis. Towards the end of their partnership, he reflected on what Hamilton represented as a person and a role model in the world outside the glam and glitter of their cocooned F1 existence.

He told reporters, 'To be honest, I think just seeing firsthand what a role model he is . . . I looked up to him the same way as all these kids look up to us. I think that's probably been the biggest life lesson that I've learned from him . . . the way you do it is important.'

A strong personal bond developed between the pair. Russell acknowledged the genuine warmth of their relationship, telling Yahoo Sports, 'We just have a good relationship. Lewis is someone whose company I really enjoy.' Hamilton echoed that sentiment, affirming their mutual respect to Sky Sports: 'I think we are a great team.

George and I have a great relationship. We discuss things and work away.'

Mercedes faced both internal pressures and occasional tension in the paddock. But Russell commented on the strain of being Hamilton's teammate, especially as outside voices tried to drive a wedge between them. 'If anything, we've grown closer together.'

He told *The Times* how he had always tried to listen and learn from Hamilton, and how that had enabled him to be his own man on the racetrack, how it had provided impetus and inspiration. 'I think you can argue that if Picasso showed an artist his work, that artist still has to recreate it . . . you can give the chef the ingredients, but they've still got to cook the meal.'

And when Hamilton left to drive for Ferrari in the 2025 season, George was quick to say he felt the loss of his mentor, but that it was now a great opportunity for him to take on the mantle of responsibility as the new number one at Mercedes. He told the *Sun*, 'Mercedes feels notably different following Lewis Hamilton's departure. He is such a huge personality, on and off the track. I also feel grateful to have had that chance to be his teammate for three years and learned so much from him but also going head-to-head with him directly for three years.'

However, mention the name Max Verstappen to Hamilton or Russell, and there's none of that respect or fondness for a fellow racer. Indeed, it's much more likely to be a shrug and grimace, such is their attitude towards the man many on the track refer to as 'Mad Max'.

Lewis's bust-ups with Max are well documented and we'll deal with that race in Abu Dhabi in 2021 – the final one of the season and the one that denied Lewis what would have been an historic eighth title – in another chapter. Suffice it to say, Hamilton felt Verstappen was sometimes a danger to himself, as well as other drivers, such was his win-at-all-costs attitude.

Hamilton versus Verstappen wasn't just a duel for the championship – it often felt like a collision of eras and personalities. From an airborne crash at Monza to a brake-test debacle in Jeddah, each dramatic moment added depth to their rivalry. Hamilton's sharp critiques – 'aggressive as hell', 'over the limit' and 'crazy man' – highlighted his views on 'Mad Max'.

The airborne crash at the Italian GP in Monza summed up their rivalry probably better than any other incident. Hamilton had attempted a daring overtake into the first turn, but Verstappen squeezed him, sending his car airborne over Hamilton's, an incident serious enough to end both their races – and potentially put Lewis's life at risk. Verstappen actually landed on top of him in the Red Bull, and but for the halo, Hamilton could have been killed.

The stewards deemed Verstappen 'predominantly at fault', resulting in a threeplace grid penalty and super licence points. Afterwards, Hamilton remarked that he was 'proud of the stewards' for making a stand on such a dangerous manoeuvre. Lewis admitted he was 'very, very fortunate' to walk away from the crash before adding, 'Thank God for the halo which saved me, and saved my neck.'

They crashed again in Saudi Arabia in 2021, with Lewis shouting on the radio, 'This guy's f*****g crazy, man! He just braketested me! I've just hit him.' He later reflected, 'I've raced a lot of drivers . . . rules kinda don't apply . . . he's over the limit, for sure.'

Even at the end of 2024, Lewis felt Max was still too aggressive, telling the press pack, 'All you have to do is go back and listen to some of my radio comments back in the day. I don't think you are seeing much difference across the years from 2021 until now; it's pretty much the same.'

As far as the newer generation of drivers go, George Russell would certainly agree with Hamilton's assessment of Verstappen. A series of run-ins since George's arrival at Mercedes in 2022 have led to his more pumped-up view of the Dutchman than with any other driver.

The first sparks in their edgy relationship can be traced back to the 2023 Azerbaijan GP sprint. A wheel-to-wheel tussle in Turn 2 resulted in contact that left Verstappen's car damaged. He later accused Russell of lacking common sense – and dubbed him 'Princess George', 'pathetic' and a 'dickhead'. Verstappen, still only 25 but already on the way to his second world title, probably expected Russell to be a shrinking violet, given he was only in his second season and had a reputation as a fairly quiet, measured guy. But George gave as good as he got, albeit in a more composed response, saying, 'I'm not just going to wave him by me, just because he's Max Verstappen in a Red Bull. I am here to fight and win.'

It set a marker for the future. He wouldn't be spoken

to like that by Verstappen, or bullied, world champion or not. As we have previously noted, Russell is confident in himself and determined and steely behind that measured, easy-going image. The tension between the pair simmered; clearly, they were hardly going to be pals, but an uneasy truce remained until the season's end.

It didn't last. The following season they clashed again, this time in Qatar. Verstappen was penalised for impeding Russell in qualifying, earning a one-place penalty which meant the latter won pole for the race itself. Verstappen was incensed and made it clear in the stewards' room afterwards that he thought he'd been robbed.

Max went on to win the race, with George coming home fourth, but the fallout continued. At the post-race press conference, Max told reporters, 'I've been in that [stewards'] meeting room many times in my life, in my career, with people that I've raced – and I've never seen someone trying to screw someone over that hard. And that for me . . . I lost all respect.'

Over to George, telling Sky Sports, 'This is not like I'm angry with Max, this is me just setting the record straight . . . I'm not going to stand here watching some guy slam me personally.'

The following week in Abu Dhabi, the final race of the calendar, he elaborated upon why he had been so angered by Verstappen.

He said, 'For me, we fight hard on the track, we fight hard in the stewards' room and it's never personal. And what happened last weekend, from my side to Max, was not personal, the same way as in the race, Max telling his team to check for Lando with the yellow flag is not personal from Max to Lando. It's part of racing, but the words he said were totally unnecessary. He's crossed a line and I'm not going to accept it, so somebody has to stand up to someone who thinks he's above the law.'

He then spoke on talkSPORT, saying, 'On Saturday night he said he was going to purposefully go out of his way to crash into me and "put me on my f***ing head in the wall". So to question somebody's integrity as a person, while saying comments like that the day before, I find is very ironic, and I'm not going to sit here and accept it. People have been bullied by Max for years now, and you can't question his driving abilities, but he cannot deal with adversity.'

His words came after Max had said he should 'f**k off' and again slammed him over the qualifying incident in Qatar.

There you have it again, the idea that – in many ways similar to Alonso with Hamilton – Verstappen, because he was world champion, had a sense of entitlement about him. That he should be treated differently, that he was above the likes of Russell who, like Hamilton in 2007, was something of a rookie still in Max's eyes.

Even after all that, the feud continued – Verstappen called him a 'loser' and dismissed his integrity. Team principals got involved – Toto Wolff defended Russell, labelling Verstappen 'yappy', and Christian Horner accusing Russell of provocation.

Even at the year-end drivers' dinner, the tension was

obvious as the pair sat at opposite ends of the table – and continued into the most recent 2025 campaign – an unspoken declaration that the feud was far from over.

In the Spanish Grand Prix, Russell made a bold attempt to pass Verstappen, which led to Verstappen driving into the side of George's car after being asked to let the Mercedes driver past, following an incident several laps earlier.

Russell felt it wasn't an accident. After the race, he complained, 'It felt very deliberate, to be honest. It's something that I've seen numerous times in sim racing and on iRacing. Never have I seen it in a Formula 1 race. So that was something new. It's a bit of a shame because Max is clearly one of the best drivers in the world. But manoeuvres like that are just totally unnecessary and let him down. It's a shame for all the young kids looking up, aspiring to be Formula 1 drivers. So, as I said, I don't know what he was thinking. In the end, I'm not going to lose sleep over it because I ultimately benefited from those antics. But you cannot deliberately crash into another driver.'

Later in the campaign, in Canada, Christian Horner joined in the 'fun', accusing George of 'goading' Max in an attempt to get him banned. He claimed Russell had braked erratically behind the safety car while George argued Max had illegally overtaken him.

But the stewards ruled in George's favour, saying, 'We are satisfied that the driver of Car 63 did not drive erratically by braking where he did or to the extent he did.' They also cleared him of unsportsmanlike conduct.

I must admit to admiring George for his unwillingness to

bend to Max's power plays. It shows an inherent strength of character to stand up to someone so powerful within F1, and for his deep will to win.

While Russell refused to suffer at the hands of Verstappen, Lando Norris refused to fall out with the Dutchman, despite their own run-ins.

As we have seen, George has publicly accused Verstappen of personal vendettas and even alleged threats and remains unapologetic and unwilling to back down over incidents.

While George is confrontational, Lando prefers a different approach – perhaps because of his more chilled nature, but also because he and Max are friends away from the grid. The pals have had multiple intense battles – Austria 2024 and Miami 2025 coming to mind as prime examples. Norris has faced aggressive defence manoeuvres from Max and even collisions, but consistently has resorted to dialogue, and held no grudge, to preserve their friendship. This approach, in turn, takes the sting out of Max. He may have acted in a hot-headed manner on the track, but off it is just as keen as Lando to retain their friendship. In February 2025, the pair laughed and joked before the start of the new season. At a pre-season press conference, they were asked about their relationship. Verstappen immediately joked, 'Yeah, it's a terrible relationship. We don't get on any more. It's taken its toll. Yeah. Big drama.' Norris joined in, adding, 'We had a fight the other day in a local pub!'

Max continued, 'We had to get escorted out. I always say, you should see the other guy . . . but he still looks good, so whatever. I think we both look forward to more of last year, more battles. I don't think it's just going to be us.'

Lando agreed. 'I think there's going to be others involved, which will make it more exciting for everyone. But yeah, I know they're going to be tough battles and I'm sure some of them are not always going to end the way I want or hopefully Max wants, but we're racing drivers.

'We get along. We've always said these kinds of things. I know everyone tries to make their own points and say what's correct and what's not correct, but we respect each other a lot and we look forward to more racing on track.'

Which is not to say Lando is a doormat when it comes to dealing with Verstappen. No, he stands up to him and calls him out but doesn't go full throttle as Russell would. In 2024's Austrian GP, they collided while battling to win the race. Both cars were damaged and Lando had to retire. Max continued on his merry way, only to be hit with a ten-second punishment for his part in the smash.

Verstappen finished fifth, despite the penalty for his reckless driving.

Norris was unhappy with his friend's driving, feeling the penalty proved Max had been at fault. He was asked after the race if it meant he had lost his respect for Max. He replied, 'It depends what he says to me. If he admits it, OK. If he says, "I was stupid," and admits he ran into me and it was reckless then a small amount of respect. Maybe.'

The pair didn't speak after the race and didn't head away from Austria in the same private jet as they normally do after races.

But the following day, they did speak after a 'cool down' period. Max would reveal days later what happened: 'To me, the only thing that I cared about is of course maintaining my relationship with Lando, because we are great friends. After the race, I said we have to just let things cool down, because emotions run high. We immediately spoke on Monday and I think we came to the conclusion that we actually really enjoyed our battle. We agree with 99 per cent of everything, so I think that's a lot already.

'Naturally, I always said to Lando, when you go for moves up the inside, outside, you can trust me that I'm not there to try and crash you out of the way, same the other way around, because we spoke about that as well. I felt everything that I did was nothing massively over the top.'

The pair's friendship was also tested in 2025 on the first lap of the Miami GP. They went wheel to wheel and Lando was forced over the kerb by Max on the first corner, dropping back to sixth. Eventually, he would work his way back up to the front and finish runner-up to teammate Piastri. McLaren team boss Andrea Stella was slightly critical of Lando for succumbing to Max's defensive move. He told Sky TV, 'On the first lap, with hindsight, it would have potentially been wiser for Lando to lift and accept he would have gained the lead later on in the race because the car was fast enough but that's with the benefit of hindsight.

'I think that was the right thing to do because Lando, in our judgement, was outside the track limits and you have to give back the track position. That's a little bit of bad luck but you have to behave and behave fairly. That could have been the risk of a penalty so it was the right thing to do.'

Norris saw it differently, criticising Verstappen for forcing him wide. In his post-race interview, he said, 'What can I say? If I don't go for it, people complain. If I go for it, people complain. So, you can't win. But it's the way it is with Max – it's crash or don't pass. Unless you get it really right and you put him in the perfect position, then you can just about get there. But I paid the price for not doing a good enough job today.'

Earlier in his career, Lando had experienced how a rookie was welcomed to a top team when he earned his seat with McLaren in 2019. There was talk in the paddock that Carlos Sainz wasn't overkeen on the arrival of the 19-year-old as his teammate. He made it clear in interviews that he viewed himself as McLaren's lead driver – although the team never formally gave him number one status. He had been driving in F1 since 2015 and delivered better early results and finished sixth in the championship that year, while Lando was 11th.

But the relationship developed and when Carlos referred to Lando as 'little brother', the public didn't see it as a put-down, more of an affectionate moniker, as Carlos himself would go on to explain. It was good to see them getting on so well in a sport that is so pressurised, physically and mentally and financially, that civility often goes missing. Then again, Lando Norris is renowned as one of F1's nice guys, even as he chases down the world title with a fierce competitiveness. Now, if only Max Verstappen would take note . . .

CHAPTER 11

EΛSY . . . ΛS 1-2-3

Sunday, 7 July 2024, is a landmark date in our story of the three top British drivers of the modern era. For, after six seasons of racing together in F1, it marked the first time they had lined up together as 1-2-3 on the starting grid. Not only that, but the historic event panned out at Silverstone, the home of British racing. It all felt very symbolic, as if we were witnessing a passing of the torch in the sport for British drivers. Hamilton, the multiple-time world champion; Norris, the charismatic rising star, and Russell, the up-and-coming talent in a new Mercedes seat – all together, embodying the depth of British talent in F1.

And it also felt as if Lewis was saying, 'Here you go, it's up to you two now to carry on the work I have laboured over for so many years. Now you both need to step up to the plate and win some championships!'

That was the feeling at lights out, but by the end of the

race, of course, it would be an altogether different tale – as Hamilton defied logic, and claims by some pundits and fans, that he was becoming yesterday's man, by actually winning the race.

George was on pole, beating Lewis to the top spot by 0.141 seconds. The previous week he had triumphed in the Austrian GP, and in front of thousands of home fans, he was understandably on a high as he celebrated pole position. He said it was a highlight of his own career to grab pole in his home GP, but also suggested it could be a turning point for the whole Mercedes team, with Lewis number two on the grid.

George commented, 'At the start of the year, we couldn't have dreamed of being on pole here. The car at the moment is feeling so good. We're riding this wave and we've got to win a race tomorrow. It's going to be tight with Lando, Max as well, but it's so exciting. I don't think Silverstone could have dreamt of three Brits in the top three.'

Lewis, who hadn't won a GP for over two years, was also happy with the way things had gone. As always, he first of all thanked the 'incredible crowd' for their support, then added, 'Three Brits in the top three. And congratulations to George, he did such an amazing job. We definitely didn't expect to be on the front row this weekend but this is huge for us. The car felt fantastic. Everyone in the garage, all our team that have come here really deserve this. The car felt great. It was about getting the tyre temperatures in the right place and sealing the deal when you knew you had the time on track.

'I think, ultimately, there was still time left on the table, which George was able to find. But I feel really confident about the car tomorrow, and with the conditions we have, we can work together to keep Lando behind.'

As for Lando . . . well, he wasn't as pleased. With the McLaren, he was now in a faster car and had expected to be on the front row, rather than the second. But he conceded it could have been worse after a mistake in Q3 meant he missed out on a final lap to improve his time. He said, 'I'm happy with P3. Three Brits lock out the top three, so pretty cool here. Good laps by George and Lewis both. They did an excellent job. A little mistake on my part at the end but P3 is still good.'

He had the belief he could make up for it on raceday. He added, 'I'm excited for the race; it's going to be a good one. We are quick, and I can bring the fight to George and Lewis. So, yes, I'm excited to put on a good show tomorrow. I hope we are going to have some good battles; I look forward to it.'

As we have seen in an earlier chapter, the race outcome was a disappointment for pole sitter, George, with him retiring on lap 24 with a water system leak. Lando started third and finished third, and Lewis chalked up his ninth win at Silverstone. It meant the history-breaking possibility of a 1-2-3 finish was not to be. However, the qualifying result and the actual potential of that 1-2-3 outcome showed that British F1 hopes were now in good hands. Hamilton had not yet passed on the baton to Norris and Russell, but he had once again shown them how it was done and had loved being part of the all-Brit lockout on the starting grid.

The lockout also highlighted just how long it had been since such a dominant all-British qualifying showing in the British GP. The last time three British drivers were P1, P2 and P3 was in 1962, when Jim Clark, John Surtees and Innes Ireland took control at Aintree, where the event was previously held. It moved to Silverstone the following year.

Grandprix.com summed up the historic 1962 lockout like this: 'For the second year running the British GP was held at Aintree and all the main teams were back in action after strikes had disrupted the appearance of Porsche at the Belgian GP and Ferrari at the French. The Italian team ran only one car for Phil Hill on this occasion. After qualifying, Jim Clark was fastest in his Lotus and shared the front row of the grid with John Surtees's Reg Parnell Racing Lola and Innes Ireland in his British Racing Partnership Lotus. Bruce McLaren (Cooper) and Graham Hill (BRM) shared the second row while French GP winner Dan Gurney was on row three in his Porsche alongside his teammate Jo Bonnier and the second BRM of Richie Ginther.'

Just as in 2024 when Russell had struggled in the actual race after a mechanical problem, so too in 1962 did Ireland, pulling out on the first lap with a bent gear lever. Clark and Surtees had better luck – in that like Norris and Hamilton, did they finish. Like Lewis, Clark notched the victory – while also setting the fastest lap. It was a typically robust showing by Jim, who led from start to finish.

Surtees also didn't disappoint, finishing runner-up despite losing second gear on lap ten.

And while there was disappointment in Ireland's non-finish, there was consolation for Brit fans in that Graham Hill was on hand to secure fourth, just outside the podium spots. Bruce McLaren took third spot.

In a distinctive, almost Pathé-news-style flashback, The British Motor Racing website summed up the importance of the last GP at Aintree, and saluted the efforts of the British drivers who took part: 'July was the month of the British Grand Prix, held in 1962 at Aintree – this race would take us past the halfway point in the Grand Prix season.

'Graham Hill's BRM had only managed fifth on the grid, with arch-rival Jim Clark in the Lotus taking pole position. Jim Clark went on to win the race; and Hill came in fourth, struggling with excessive tyre wear as the race progressed. However, in the overall scheme of things, there was promise and optimism; Hill was leading the Drivers' Championship; ahead of Jim Clark by one point.

'In the Constructors' Championship, BRM were in second place, behind Lotus by one point. There was all to play for, and the contribution of Hill's BRM teammate Richie Ginther was a huge part of this – and his third place in the French Grand Prix at Rheims when Hill's BRM failed to finish just shows how important Richie's contribution was to the eventual Constructors' Championship victory.'

Motor Sport magazine was similarly typically British in their formality as they reviewed the race after it finished, 'On lap 67 Clark lapped Brabham and steadily the race ran itself out, with Clark about to lap Graham Hill in the closing laps. However, Clark decided to be a gentleman and he eased up and let Hill remain on the same lap, but Taylor, who was all the time following Clark, thought differently and raced on, passing them both and thus being only one lap behind his teammate instead of two.

'So, the British Grand Prix finished, a splendid victory for Jimmy Clark and the Lotus 25, unchallenged from start to finish, but not at all what had been expected. Surtees finished a firm second in the Lola, which proved itself very raceworthy and a future winner given the right circumstances, and in third place was McLaren in the Cooper V8, having driven a typical sound and sure race, while Graham Hill came home fourth, the last to complete the full race distance.'

Silverstone in 2024 and Aintree in 1962 witnessed the most recent all-British front-row lockouts at a British GP. However, in between those home events, there was a similar story at the 1968 South African GP – when Jim Clark took pole at his final F1 race, ahead of Graham Hill and Jackie Stewart.

In the race itself, Clark roared home first in his Lotus 49-Ford. He controlled the race brilliantly, leading 73 of the 80 laps, and claimed his 25th career win – a record at the time. To ice the cake, he also set the fastest lap.

Graham Hill, also in a Lotus 49-Ford, finished 25.3 seconds behind his teammate to secure second place, making it a Lotus 1-2. Jackie Stewart, in the Matra-Ford, had qualified third but retired on lap 43 due to engine failure.

Tragically, the race became Clark's final Grand Prix victory and appearance. He died in a Formula 2 race at

Hockenheim just three months later, on 7 April 1968. Hill then went on to win the 1968 World Championship. Stewart, after a slow start, emerged later in the season as a dominant force with Matra.

Clark died when his Lotus-Cosworth Formula 2 car crashed into a tree at Hockenheim. The precise reason for the crash remains uncertain. Theories include mechanical failure, suspension issues or a sudden tyre deflation on the damp track. His death stunned the racing world. Clark was considered one of the greatest and safest drivers of his era. His passing intensified the push for better safety measures in the sport.

In the documentary, *Jim Clark: The Quiet Champion*, Jackie Stewart paid tribute to the man voted third in a BBC list of the best F1 drivers of all time. Jackie said, 'He was so smooth, he was so clean – he drove with such finesse. He never bullied a racing car; he sort of caressed it into doing the things he wanted it to do.'

The Jim Clark Trust summed up the loss of such a great man, as well as a great British driver: 'He was 32. There were no witnesses. Time catastrophically stood still. Colin Chapman and his teammate Graham Hill were devastated. The world was shocked by his death. Jim was considered to be one of the safest, most skilled and naturally gifted drivers and his peers did not think that driver error had caused the crash. A deflated rear tyre was widely blamed and accepted as the cause for the incident.

'Hill would go on to claim the Formula 1 World Championship in 1968, which he dedicated to his friend's memory. Fellow racing driver Chris Amon summoned up the sentiments of many others at the time, "If it could happen to him, what chance do the rest of us have? I think we all felt that. It seemed like we'd lost our leader."'

Clark once explained what drove him to push for glory at high speed, yet at the same time remain well within control of the car. He said, 'The supreme attraction of motor racing to me is driving a car as near the physical limit as possible without stepping over it. I have always recognised and respected the safety limits for myself and other drivers, and I would far rather lose a race any day than overstep myself or my car.'

This quote certainly evokes the spirit and mindset of Lewis Hamilton. He knows the limits of his car and himself, and has always pushed himself to the edge, but not over it like, say, Schumacher or Verstappen. Paddy Lowe, former McLaren engineering director, had praised Hamilton for his ability to 'tame a car', and to handle rear instability problems that would drive other drivers mad.

Like Clark, Hamilton has been the fairest of sportsmen and a great example to the likes of Norris and Russell – just as Jim was for Lewis.

After Clark's death in 1968, Graham Hill wrote a wonderful reflective piece on his friend's life for *Sports Illustrated* magazine. He focused on that fateful day at Hockenheim and paid tribute to Clark for his talent, presence and being the best of the best, 'I am sure that it wasn't Jimmy's fault at Hockenheim. Everyone was taking that curve flat out, and Jimmy was the best man in the race

– and best in the world. He was that because he just had all the requirements; he was a natural athlete with very good muscular coordination and a very good eye. He had a springy step; he was light on his feet. He had rhythm. His judgement was excellent, and his reactions were very fast.

'He was also particularly competitive, particularly aggressive, but he combined this with an extremely good sense of what not to do. One can be over-thrusting – aggressive to the point of being dangerous. Well, this Jimmy was not. But he was a fighter, a fighter that you could never shake off. He invariably shot into the lead and killed off the others, building up a lead that sapped their will to win . . . Jimmy, in his era, was unsurpassed.'

It would be a cruel irony that just under a decade later, Graham Hill would also leave us. Another British genius on the F1 track was taken away far too early. Graham died in a plane crash on 29 November 1975. The BBC reported it like this on the day itself: 'One of Britain's greatest motor racing drivers has been killed in a plane crash in south-east England. Graham Hill, 46, who retired from the sport in July 1975, was killed instantly along with the four other occupants in his Piper Aztec – all members of the Embassy Hill team. Hill was piloting the plane when he clipped a row of trees on Arkley golf course in Hertfordshire, just before 2200 GMT.'

Around 3,000 people attended his funeral in St Albans, Hertfordshire, on 5 December.

An inquest into his death found he was flying only 60 ft above the ground when the plane hit the tree but did not realise because of the poor visibility. The coroner returned verdicts of accidental death on all six people on the plane.

Hill was the only man to win the Triple Crown of the Formula 1 title, Le Mans 24-hour race and the Indianapolis 500. A lovely tribute was provided by formula1.com's Gerald Donaldson, who wrote: 'Graham Hill's iron-willed determination, fierce pride and great courage enabled him to overcome the odds against more naturally gifted drivers. None of them was more popular with the public than the moustachioed extrovert with the quick wit, who loved the limelight, was a natural entertainer and became one of the first Formula 1 media stars. His fans remained loyal, even when he damaged his reputation by racing too long past his prime. Millions were shocked when he was killed, not in a racing car, but at the controls of his plane.'

It meant that two of the three Brits who had been part of the British 1-2-3 in South Africa in 1968 had died tragically – Jim Clark in an F2 car at Hockenheim and Graham Hill while flying a light aircraft.

However, the Hill family's racing lineage continued with Graham's son, Damon, who followed his father into Formula 1 racing and won the World Championship in 1996.

That neatly ties up the links between the 2024 British GP 1-2-3 front row contenders, and those of 1962 at Aintree and 1968 in South Africa. Pacesetters and pioneers in their own eras, and all proud Britons.

Now let's shift the focus back on the current three battling for glory, and who are the main focus of this book – Hamilton, Norris and Russell – and examine the seasons they have raced together as a trio. That's 2019, 2020 and 2021 for the purpose of this chapter. We'll be focusing on memorable highs and lows for each driver. The years 2022, 2023 and 2024 are covered in the next chapter.

The year 2025 makes up our final chapter, zooming in on that year while also having one eye on the future.

In 2019, the gulf between Hamilton and the other two was cavernous. He was a British icon who was already widely regarded as a superstar and ambassador for the sport, with journalists praising his impact both on and off the grid. He was arguably at his peak and would win his sixth Drivers' Championship that year, finishing ahead of teammate Valtteri Bottas and Red Bull's Max Verstappen. Mercedes would also win the Constructors' Championship. Norris and Russell both explicitly acknowledged Hamilton as someone they looked up to, with Norris also benefiting from Hamilton's friendly words and warmth, even if informally.

Both he and Russell saw Hamilton as the role model they wanted to be – his success and respect within the sport was an aspirational target, and they knew he was there if they ever needed advice. He was the godfather of British F1, both on the track and off it.

It was Lando's rookie season, and he finished a creditable 11th in the Drivers' Championship, in the McLaren, on 49 points. His best finish was sixth, which he achieved in both Austria and Bahrain. He did well, showing consistent pace and aggression against his experienced teammate, Carlos Sainz, who finished sixth overall.

For George, it was also a rookie season, but he would fare much worse than Lando, basically because he was in a Williams, the slowest car on the grid that year. He finished 20th in the Drivers' Championship (last among full-time drivers), with no points. His best finish was 11th but he showed his mettle by regularly outperforming his teammate Robert Kubica in qualifying.

In terms of highlights and lows in 2019, Hamilton won the British GP at Silverstone in front of his home fans, even setting the fastest lap on the final lap with old tyres. The win meant he had beaten Jim Clark and Alain Prost as the driver with the most British Grand Prix victories, and it took him 31 points clear at the top of the driver standings.

Afterwards, he enjoyed his traditional love-in with the thousands of fans who had come to cheer him on, telling them, 'Oh, what a day – I love you, Silverstone. You think you'd get used to something like that, but it feels like the first time.'

A low would have been at Hockenheim. He was poorly, crashed into barriers and picked up a penalty for an incorrect pit-lane entry. He crashed on lap 29 at Turn 16, damaging his front wing and forcing an unscheduled pit stop. Finishing 11th in the rain, it was his worst performance of an otherwise fine year. Afterwards, as some consolation for an awful afternoon in Germany, he was promoted to ninth place after Alfa Romeo drivers Kimi Räikkönen and Antonio Giovinazzi were given 30-second time penalties. Lewis summed it all up like this: 'This has been one of the most difficult races we've had as a team for a long time.

I thought I had the race under control, but we took a risk going out on slicks and the race fell apart from there.

'I went wide at Turn 16 and it was like ice out there, then hit the wall and damaged my wing. I made a mistake and paid the price. I was in the lead and then finished P11. I'm not even sure how, but that's very painful and I'm just glad it's over. It's hard to perform when you're not at 100 per cent. I need to make sure I'm fit and healthy again in time for the next race. You live and you learn from days like this.'

Lando's 2019 highlight came in Bahrain, where he finished sixth in what was only his second F1 race. He was pleased with his first points in the sport, but felt he could have done even better, a sure sign of his determination and ambition even at this early stage.

After the race, he said, 'The pace, especially in the first stint, was very good. I think I could be a bit more attacking. I was a bit soft sometimes on Turn 1. I think I could have gone for an overtake but I didn't want to risk a lock-up or something silly because I knew I had pace and it's a long race.

'I'm happy not just for myself but for the team. It's my second race; sixth is very good.'

His low point would be at Spa when the McLaren's engine failed on the final lap. He had been running fifth, but was classified 11th, missing out on the points. A consolation was that he was awarded Driver of the Day, but it still hurt. He told Sky Sports F1, 'I was on for my best result, and as a team it was our joint best result, from what Carlos [Sainz] has achieved, so things were looking so good. Things were looking up as for a while I haven't had a great result for myself.

'Whatever was giving me power, stopped giving me power. That's the simple way of putting it. Other people are in worse situations than I am, so I can't be that disappointed.' For George Russell, there would be few highlights in 2019, usually low points or, given his positivity despite having the slowest car on the track, learning and evolution moments. If there was a high, it was possibly his 11th place finish at Hockenheim, his best result of the season – and just one place from finishing in the points. He had crossed the line in 13th but was moved up two spots – as Hamilton had also been – due to the time penalties of Räikkönen and Giovinazzi.

He said of the rain-lashed race, 'It was extremely challenging. It wasn't ideal conditions for anyone out there and it was a long race. We should have taken slicks under the penultimate safety car, but I think we took the conservative approach when we should have maybe rolled the dice.

'There were 13 or 14 other drivers on the grid who didn't do that so it's not exactly that we made the wrong call, but we had the opportunity to make the right call. We kept it on the black stuff when a lot of people didn't, and it was the best result of the year. It seems OK but there was a chance for more.'

Pinpointing a real low that season, well, maybe Japan. He said qualifying was his 'best' of the year, but the race was his 'worst'. In terms of the actual race result, his comment sounds illogical as he qualified lower than he finished, 18th and 16th respectively – but race conditions were extremely challenging, with both the wind and the car. George said the braking system had been 'atrocious' as he battled on the track in Suzuka. 'We had some brake issues throughout which made it quite difficult. It was definitely one of the tougher races of the season.' He had even considered retiring the car during the race, such was the problem.

He summed up his weekend as a challenge, but one he had enjoyed, 'Qualifying was incredibly tricky, especially through the Esses. It made it unpredictable, but I gave it everything and I think overall, we overachieved so I was pleased with that. It was an incredibly tricky race for us. I have mixed feelings, but I can be satisfied. When I woke this morning, I felt fresh and I did the job.'

Dave Robson, Williams's senior race engineer, gave George a pat on the back. He said, 'Qualifying was held in dry but very gusty conditions, making it difficult for everybody. George did a good job in qualifying, finishing very close to Perez. For his first experience of Suzuka it was a tricky challenge, which he rose to very well.'

The year 2020 brought fresh challenges for George, Lewis and Lando. Lewis would continue his all-conquering run in the Mercedes, George would show he did have what it takes to earn a top seat as he stood in for Lewis in Sakhir, and Lando once again delivered the pace to suggest he was well on his way to being a top, top driver.

Hamilton soared into the record books by winning his seventh world title, equalling Michael Schumacher's historic number. He won 11 of 17 races and clinched the championship at the Turkish GP, finishing P1 in tricky wet-dry conditions. But he would test positive for Covid prior to the Sakhir GP, missing the race and witnessing for the first time that George Russell might not only have what it takes to become a teammate, but become an eventual worthy successor at Mercedes.

Lando finished ninth in the 2020 Drivers' Championship with 97 points. He claimed his maiden Formula 1 podium at the Austrian Grand Prix (P3) and consistently scored points for McLaren, helping the team – along with teammate Sainz – secure third place in the Constructors' Championship.

At Williams, it was another bleak season for George. He finished 18th in the Drivers' Championship, with no points. But he did out-qualify his new teammate Nicholas Latifi at every race (20–0 across this year and 2021). He also made waves when he stood in for Hamilton at the Sakhir GP. Starting P2 on the grid in the Mercedes, he led for much of the race. As we have previously noted, only a Mercedes pit stop blunder and a late puncture denied him a podium, or even victory. He still finished ninth, notching the first points of his F1 career.

Turning to highlights and lowlights, for Lewis, the obvious high was securing his historic seventh title, which he did in spectacular fashion at Istanbul on 15 November 2020. Starting sixth on a rain-soaked, slippery track, many saw danger, but for Hamilton, arguably the best ever F1 driver in wet conditions, it was perfect. After early struggles, he switched to intermediates, managed them brilliantly, and built a commanding lead while rivals faltered. His dominance was such that he crossed the line over 30 seconds ahead, sealing his place in F1 history.

He said, 'I'm definitely a bit lost for words. I have to start by saying a huge thank you to all our guys here, and back at both our factories. I wouldn't be able to be here if I didn't join this team and the journey we've been on has been monumental. I'm so proud. I've got to say thank you to my family. We dreamed of this when we were young, watching the Grand Prix, and this is way, way beyond our dreams. It's so important for kids – dream the impossible. You've got to work for it, chase it, and never give up or doubt yourself.'

He had won the title with three races to spare and was now dubbed the GOAT (Greatest of all Time) after drawing level with Schumacher. Some argued he was actually only the joint GOAT, but the stats suggested he stood alone. Even back in 2020, he had more race wins, pole positions and podium finishes than Schumacher. Of course, you could argue that Michael might have carried on winning but for his tragic accident, but we will never know.

And the facts suggest not. Schumacher was left in a critical condition after the skiing accident in the French ski resort of Méribel on 29 December 2013. The then 44-year-old had just retired from F1 for a second time at the end of the previous season, having returned to the sport with Mercedes between 2010 and 2012. So it was unlikely he would have returned for a third time.

Lewis has never suggested he is superior to Michael. He refers to him as a legend and is humble and respectful enough to accept that he will always be an icon of the sport. There is no competitive edge or desire to personally claim that GOAT acclaim on Hamilton's side. In 2024, Lewis penned a tribute as the foreword to a book about Schumacher, *World Championship Cars: Michael Schumacher*. He wrote, 'Michael is among the legends in our sport. When you grow up with a passion for motorsport, you always look up at specific people, and without doubt Michael was a role model for young drivers.

'His speed, his work morals, his determination and consistency – the length of his career and his top performance can only be admired. When it comes to Michael's legacy, however, I focus on him as a person rather than a competitor. It's not about titles or trophies, but about the family that he and [his wife] Corinna created together. Their greatness, their humility and their sincerity say much more about Michael's values than I ever could.'

One of Hamilton's few lows in 2020 came at Monza on 6 September. After storming to pole and dominating early on, a pit lane closure – after Kevin Magnussen's Haas broke down on the outside of the first corner – caught Mercedes off guard. They called Hamilton in, unaware the lane was closed, and he entered it unknowingly. The result was a ten-second stop/go penalty that dropped him to last. Yet, he charged back to finish P7. 'Honestly, I didn't see the boards,' he said afterwards. 'I take responsibility for that. It's frustrating, but that's racing. I didn't even know the pit lane was closed. But I'm grateful I could still get back into the points.'

Mercedes boss Toto Wolff conceded, 'The decisions that

were taken were highly unusual – but they were absolutely within the rules. With Lewis and the penalty, it was a weird sequence of events. We should have spotted earlier that the pit lane was closed; by the time that we did, the car was entering the pit lane.'

Lando Norris's standout moment of the 2020 season came at the season-opening Austrian Grand Prix on 5 July at the Red Bull Ring in Spielberg. He qualified P4 in the McLaren, showing strong pace throughout. Lando maintained the pace he had shown in qualifying during the race itself. In the final lap, he overtook Sergio Perez and set the fastest lap, earning an extra championship point. He crossed the line in fourth, but leapfrogged Hamilton into third after Lewis received a five-second penalty for contact with Alex Albon, ten laps earlier.

At just 20 years and 235 days old, Norris became the third-youngest driver in F1 history to stand on the podium, behind Max Verstappen and Lance Stroll.

After the race, he said, 'I'm speechless. I think there were a few points in the race where I thought I fudged it up quite a bit. I dropped to fifth with a few laps to go; Carlos was almost getting past me. I managed to get past Perez, and I ended up on the podium.

'It was a long race, but I kept going. I was trying to give it my all; it was a pretty cool last few laps, having to push as much as I can – you can tell I'm a little bit out of breath. I'm so happy, so proud of the team. Considering where we were a few years ago, from last year to now, it's a pretty cool achievement and I'm proud to be part of it all.'

Now pundits and fans were starting to sit up and take notice of the boy from Bristol as a real contender.

The podium finish was a personal milestone – and also laid down a marker that McLaren was finally re-emerging as a force to be reckoned with.

After the high, inevitably perhaps a low, one of the unfortunate facts of life, and Lando delivered a low blow of his own in the Portuguese GP in October. He was riled by events on the track in the race and afterwards didn't come out of an interview at all well; an interview ironically about one of the key subjects of this book.

Lando was asked to give his thoughts, and no doubt, some praise for Lewis Hamilton, who had just set the record for the most career wins. Two weeks after equalling Michael Schumacher's 91 wins in 2006, Hamilton had won his 92nd in Portugal. But Lando said of the achievement, 'He's in a car which should win every race, basically. He has to beat one or two other drivers, that's it.'

Factually, of course, that is probably not far off the mark. Although, to be fair, the likes of Hamilton and Verstappen have often made a mockery of that general conception by regularly beating teammates and even winning when their cars had suffered 'off days'.

But the comment sounded disrespectful and mean-spirited. On the Tuesday following the race, Lando made amends, writing on Twitter (X), 'I owe an apology. I've been stupid and careless with some things I've said lately in media and interviews and haven't shown the respect I should have to certain people. I'm not that kind of person, so I know

I should apologise to them but also everyone reading/ listening. Sorry.'

F1 fans hadn't made a song and dance about his comments and many backed him. But one fan made a perceptive comment about why it could have been seen as perhaps an elitist and entitled jibe – given the relative hardships Lewis suffered to even make it to F1, compared with Lando's more privileged route. The fan wrote in reply, 'There are always the elite teams that dominate F1, it's just been more top heavy the last two decades. (Schumacher, Vettel, Hamilton). We all know Stroll is a rich dilettante. But Lando, I'd love to see you try and walk a mile in Lewis's shoes as a young kid trying to make it.'

The cause of Lando's unusual mutterings was clear: he had been asked directly after a race in which he had lost the chance to pick up points. He had got off to a decent start but ended up battling with Lance Stroll for seventh spot at Turn 1, resulting in a collision. The McLaren was damaged and Lando had to pit for repairs and by race end had finished in a disappointing P13.

That frustration seeped through in the questioning by the media and led to the Hamilton faux pas.

A few days later, before qualifying at the next GP in Imola, Lando expanded upon his regret and admitted he had apologised personally to Lewis. 'I have a lot of respect for [his 92 wins] and I just didn't choose those words to put it into context. I also apologised to Lewis himself; I messaged him at the time. I don't know if he knew about it at the time but I never meant to say something like that in a bad way or

20

put any bad light on him at all. I respect everything he's done to achieve what he's done. It's incredible no matter what.

'It's just the way I put it was just not the way I wanted to put it across. I said what I said, I apologised and I've just got to move on.'

I was told that Lewis was fine about the whole incident and was never upset or bothered. He understood it was a heat of the moment reaction and not said in disrespect. Indeed, as we have noted throughout this book, both Norris and George Russell had and have said how much they do admire Hamilton, as a man and a racer, and that they hold him up as an example of what can be achieved as a British driver.

For George, 2020's highlight was undoubtedly his stand-in success for Hamilton at Sakhir. As we saw with Lando's apology to Lewis, it was starting to become clearer that here was a British triumvirate who were ready to make joint headlines in F1, albeit in unexpected ways at this stage. Their paths were beginning to entwine as success and ambition took hold of all three, albeit at differing levels.

George's Sakhir joys have been covered in an earlier chapter.

His low in 2020? I'd say Imola in November when he ruined his own chance of gaining his first points for Williams and himself in F1.

It was the first race held back at the Autodromo Enzo e Dino Ferrari since 2006, but Russell would be glad when he was on a plane out of Italy. Williams was still one of the slowest teams, but Russell had been consistently outperforming teammate Nicholas Latifi in both qualifying and races. On lap 51 of 63, Russell was running P10. Then the safety car was deployed after Max Verstappen retired with a tyre failure.

Under the safety car, on cold and worn hard tyres, George was weaving aggressively to try to maintain temperature on the run to Acque Minerali. But as he applied throttle and changed gear, the rear of the Williams snapped.

He spun into a wall, damaging the car and, as it was under the safety car, had no chance to recover. Russell retired from the race, missing out on a potential P9 or P10 finish. Afterwards, he said, 'That's the biggest mistake I've ever made in my career. I'm really sorry to the team. There are no excuses. It hurts so much. I had the race under control, and I just threw it away.'

And so on to 2021 . . . and the season that arguably ended Lewis Hamilton's era of dominance. He would lose his grip on the Drivers' Championship title in the cruellest of circumstances and, at the same time, some pundits and fans began to talk excitedly about Norris and Russell now emerging as torch bearers for Hamilton's throne as the top Brit in F1; a new era of younger talent set to oust the legend. Those thoughts proved fanciful, although sure, the duo were growing stronger by the year – and George especially would benefit enormously when he took Valtteri Bottas's seat at Mercedes.

No, the narrative of Norris and Russell as Britain's next front-runners would evolve more gradually. It would become more evident in 2024 and beyond, as both started to deliver stronger results and Hamilton's title years appeared to be behind him.

For now, in 2021, the headline news, and main rivalry, remained that of Hamilton and his Dutch nemesis, Verstappen.

Hamilton notched eight race wins that season and should have clinched his eighth world title, but for a clanger dropped by the race director in Abu Dhabi. His title hopes were dashed in a final-lap showdown that left fans – and Lewis – heartbroken. It meant he finished second in the championship, with 387.5 points, with Max lifting his first title.

It was the year Lando Norris came of age, with four podiums and his first pole position in Russia. His drive in Sochi was nearly flawless until late-race rain and a gamble on tyres cost him a maiden win. He finished sixth in the championship with 160 points.

For George Russell, the season was another in making the best of a limited car. Driving for Williams, he earned the nickname 'Mr. Saturday' in a nod to his excellent qualifying performances. His P2 in Belgium – where rain shortened the race to just two laps – provided him with a first podium. That, plus 16 points and a string of standout drives, confirmed to Mercedes that he was a real contender for the seat that Bottas would vacate. Lewis's season highlights came at Silverstone, which we have covered in an earlier chapter, where he won after yet another run-in with Verstappen – and Brazil.

Hamilton arrived in Brazil facing two big setbacks. First came a disqualification from Friday qualifying for a rear wing DRS infringement, stripping him of pole and sending him to the back for Saturday's Sprint.

Then, a five-place grid penalty for a new engine meant even if he recovered in the Sprint, he'd still be pushed down for Sunday's Grand Prix.

But true to character, he set about righting the wrongs. In the Sprint, he carved through the field from 20th to fifth in just 24 laps.

Then came the GP on Sunday. Starting tenth, he hunted down rivals, culminating in a fierce wheel-to-wheel battle with Verstappen. At Turn 4, Verstappen forced both wide, but Hamilton regrouped, attacked again and made it stick. It was a brilliant win for the Brit. Afterwards, Mercedes boss Toto Wolff paid tribute, saying, 'Overall, I definitely rate that among the best-ever performances I have ever seen from Lewis.'

Sky F1 commentator, former F1 driver Martin Brundle, added that it was 'one of the greatest drives I've ever seen in Formula 1'.

And Hamilton, almost overcome with emotion, said, 'What a race. The team did an amazing job. I was pushing as hard as I could. From last on the grid and then another five-place penalty was the hardest weekend I've had. My dad reminded me of 2004, F3 in Bahrain, where I started last and then tenth and finished first.

'Coming into the weekend, I never thought we would be able to close the gap like we did today; things kept going against us. But it just shows that you have to keep pushing and never, ever stop fighting.'

Looking back on the race in 2023, Lewis told reporters, 'I think for sure my best race ever and probably the most special race of my career. I was so proud to hold this flag [the Brazilian] on the podium. Growing up, I'd always loved Ayrton Senna; I'd watch him when he is carrying a flag. I'd qualified on pole, and then I got disqualified for a wing that was 0.02 millimetres out or something crazy like that. I remember that in that moment for me, my heart just sunk.

'I knew that I had to win every race, and I remember at that moment I thought it was over, I can't win this World Championship.

'With all the work we had done through the year, I just felt so deflated and so powerless. And somehow, it's been something that I've been able to do my whole career; somehow, I was able to move on.

'There is nothing you can do about the past, you move forwards, you can do this. I just stayed in the evening and just put it aside. I did all the studying, I came back the next day, and I drove from last to first.

'And I saw one of the marshals holding the [Brazilian] flag, and I stopped and grabbed it. That was just one of the most special moments, when I held the flag up on the podium.'

He said it was to let all his Brazilian fans know how much he appreciated them: 'I acknowledge you; I appreciate Ayrton and love Ayrton. I always have since I was a kid. I was hoping that I would lift up the nation in some way even though I wasn't from Brazil, except now I am Brazilian.'

That was some high, but the lowest of lows would follow at Abu Dhabi in the race that would decide whether he won that eighth title, or not. Heading into the final race of the season, he and Verstappen were tied on 369.5 points. It was a real winner-takes-all showdown and Lewis pulled away from the Dutchman and was on course to secure the crown. Then, disaster struck.

Ironically, given Lewis's admiration for Michael Schumacher, it would be the German's son, Mick, who would contribute to Hamilton's downfall. In his final outing with the Haas racing team, Mick collided with Nicholas Latifi, seven laps from the end.

Red Bull used the introduction of the safety car to give Verstappen new soft tyres. Lewis, meanwhile, was still on his old hard compound tyres.

That wasn't just why Lewis would lose out. Everything changed when race director Michael Masi decided to allow five lapped cars between Lewis and Max to unlap themselves – and then restarted the race with only one lap remaining. With the tyres advantage, Max soon roared past Lewis to win his first title and deny Lewis the eighth that should have been his. Toto Wolff was furious at the 'unjustness' of it all, while a grief-stricken Lewis was visibly distraught and said, 'This has been manipulated, man.'

He sat in his Mercedes for several minutes after the race and then had to be comforted trackside by his dad, Anthony. Mercedes appealed the result but the F1 authorities were not for turning. Masi had, unintentionally, incorrectly applied the rulebook and he would ultimately lose his job, but that was little consolation to the robbed Hamilton and Mercedes.

Lewis was devastated and did not speak to the press after the race. He also boycotted the end of season prize-giving spectacular and returned home feeling unsure about his future. It would be the following February before he revealed his feelings over the loss. He admitted he had 'unplugged and switched off' to escape the furore and added that he had 'lost a little bit of faith' in the sport's administration.

Then, the battling spirit that had brought him so far re-emerged, as he added, 'Moments like this might define others' careers but I refuse to let this define mine. I focused on being the best I can be and coming back stronger.'

But Red Bull were getting stronger, as was Max Verstappen, and although he didn't realise it at the time, Hamilton's hold on the title trophy was coming to an end. More of that in the next chapter.

For Lando Norris, one high moment in 2021 came as he won that first ever F1 pole in Russia. He led for most of the race but finished seventh after sticking to slicks in the rain while others – including winner Hamilton – switched to intermediates.

Perhaps his biggest high was at the Italian GP in Monza. He finished second in a McLaren 1-2, behind teammate Daniel Ricciardo. It represented McLaren's first win since 2012 and their first 1-2 since Canada in 2010. Many called it a 'coming of age moment' for Lando and McLaren. He had proved he could challenge for the title and the team had shown they now had a car that was good enough to propel him there.

The shadow of Hamilton would once again be cast

across Norris, an indication of the crossing of paths as we advance to a conclusion in this book's narrative. It was the dual elimination of the champion and Verstappen that opened the door for Lando and Daniel. Lewis had just come from the pits on lap 26 and ended up side by side with Max. The pair made contact, with Max's Red Bull catapulted high above the ground and finishing on top of Lewis's Mercedes.

After taking P2, Lando said, 'It's incredible. The main thing it means for me is our result as a team. Whether I'm second, third or first, I think the best thing is just having that 1-2 for the team, securing the maximum points and it's just such a cool feeling to be part of this. I'm happy for Daniel and the whole team because it's a pretty awesome achievement for all of us.'

And so to George Russell, and how his 2021 season panned out. As far as lows go, he'd probably concede that his crash with Bottas at Imola was a day to forget. George, in the Williams, collided with Valtteri, in the Mercedes, on Lap 32 while attempting an overtake at high speed on the approach to Turn 1.

The track was damp and as Russell moved right, his car touched the grass, causing him to lose control. Both cars smashed into the barriers at high speed. Russell confronted Bottas trackside, slapping his helmet and accusing him of a dangerous move. Bottas, in turn, blamed Russell for the crash.

The stewards reviewed the crash and ruled it a racing incident, meaning neither driver was officially at fault. Yet the significance of the moment wasn't lost on pundits. Not just for the race, but also for the growing speculation that Russell would replace Bottas at Mercedes the following season. Which, of course, would draw a strand within this book as he would become a teammate of Hamilton.

The day after the race, Russell, to some people's surprise it must be said, apologised on social media: 'Sunday wasn't my proudest day. I knew it would be one of the best opportunities to score points this season and, when these points matter as much as they do to us right now, sometimes you take risks. It didn't pay off and I have to take responsibility for that. Having had time to reflect on what happened afterwards, I know I should have handled the whole situation better.

'Emotions can run high in the heat of the moment and mine got the better of me. I apologise to Valtteri, my team, and anyone who felt let down by my actions. That's not who I am and I expect more from myself, as I know others expect from me. I have learned some tough lessons this weekend and will come out of this a better driver and a better person for the experience.'

Some pundits said it was an exercise in damage limitation. That was because Toto Wolff had criticised him over the crash, calling it 'bullshit' when George had seemingly implied Bottas had deliberately defended his position aggressively because he feared George may take his seat. Toto had added, 'The whole situation should have never happened. George should have never launched into this manoeuvre, considering that the track was drying up.'

But George had more luck at Spa that season, finishing P2

in the Belgian GP. It was his first Formula 1 podium finish, and arguably the defining moment of his Williams career. Williams had not stood on the podium since 2017 – with Lance Stroll in Azerbaijan – and not in the top two since 2014. Russell had to do it the hard way as the whole weekend was rain-soaked. He achieved a 'lap of his life' in qualifying, putting the Williams FW43B on P2, just 0.321s behind Verstappen's Red Bull. The achievement confirmed the 'Mr. Saturday' nickname he had gained because of his efforts in qualifying on Saturdays was well earned and justified.

Torrential rain on raceday meant the start was delayed multiple times. After more than three hours of waiting, only two laps were run behind the safety car, just enough for the race to be classified under FIA rules. Verstappen was declared winner, Russell second and Hamilton third. Less than three-quarters of race distance had been covered, so only half points were awarded. Some pundits reckoned Russell had, therefore, only earned his first podium by default. But others rightly pointed out that he'd earned it because of his qualifying excellence.

George was in agreement with the latter. Afterwards, he commented, 'It actually counted, it actually counted, so a little celebration tonight, I'm sure. My whole team deserves it as there has been so much hard work going into it over the last few years and there has not really been anything to show for it or prove for it.

'We absolutely nailed it yesterday and here we are standing on the podium. I can tell you I didn't expect that this year, that's for sure. For the whole team, it's a massive result. For us to be standing on this podium, it doesn't really matter how we achieved it; standing on this podium is a huge result for us.

'I believe the number of points we scored in Hungary were probably enough to have secured that eighth in the Constructors' Championship.

'But it probably takes even more pressure off now, to go out, really put everything on the line, maybe try some more extreme things, see if we can learn anything more. There's no reason why we can't score more points.'

With hindsight, his praise and encouragement for the team could have been down to already knowing, or believing, he was about to move on to Mercedes: a farewell thank you. No matter, life was about to change dramatically for George Russell – and Lewis Hamilton and Lando Norris – as the F1 cars were stowed away at the end of 2021. The 2022 season would bring more surprise ups, and downs, for all three British stars.

CHAPTER 12

THE PENDULUM SWINGS

In 2022, Lewis Hamilton endured his worst ever season in F1. The seven-time world champion secured no wins, finished sixth in the Drivers' Championship and wasn't even the best driver in his own team. No, George Russell, for the first time, overshadowed his illustrious teammate, finishing fourth in the title race. George notched 275 points over the season, Lewis 240.

OK, in podium counts, Lewis outnumbered George by nine to eight. But George clinched victory in Brazil, and Lewis was the first to admit that George rather than he deserved the accolades that season. George's single victory, plus his finishing ahead of Lewis in the championship, would leave 2022 feeling like a symbolic passing-of-the-torch moment inside Mercedes.

As for Lando Norris, well, this wasn't the Lando we would encounter in 2025, far from it. The reason? The car.

The MCL36 was a major disappointment, with aerodynamic and handling issues and braking problems. Plus, like Mercedes, McLaren struggled with the new 2022 ground-effect regulations. The rules reintroduced ground-effect aerodynamics, aiming to improve overtaking by reducing turbulent air.

They eventually tamed the porpoising (bouncing), but the car wasn't adaptable across different tracks. And while Ferrari and Red Bull brought major upgrade packages to boost their cars, McLaren's development pace lagged.

McLaren's dilemmas were highlighted by their fifth-place finish in the Constructors' Championship at the end of the campaign, on 159 points and behind Red Bull, Ferrari, Mercedes and Alpine.

But looking at the credit side for Lando, he finished on 122 points to teammate Ricciardo's 37, a considerable gulf. And he landed their only podium all season with a third-place spot at Imola. He was also the only driver outside the 'big three' of the era – Red Bull, Ferrari and Mercedes – to make the podium in 2022.

So, what happened to Hamilton?

You don't have to be a genius to work out that part of his problem that season was mired in the previous season or, more precisely, the final race of 2021, and that cruel loss to Verstappen that cost him his eighth title. One he should have won but for a terrible mistake by the race director at Abu Dhabi.

Lewis suffered a long emotional hangover. An F1 source said: 'He was shell-shocked by what had happened.

Everyone knew that the eighth title should have been his. He was distraught afterwards and it really did affect him for months.'

It would be the following February before Hamilton revealed his feelings over the loss. He admitted he had 'unplugged and switched off' to escape the furore and added that he had 'lost a little bit of faith' in the sport's administration.

But while Verstappen had won his first championship by default, Red Bull as a team were getting stronger and the car faster. The supremacy that Mercedes, and Lewis, had enjoyed for years was coming to an end.

Max was not only the new champ on the block; his team would also prove to be champions, giving him the fastest car on the grid. Lewis Hamilton's period of dominance was over.

And reigning constructors' champions Mercedes could only finish third, their lone victory coming in São Paulo, courtesy of Russell. Lewis's fellow Brit had replaced Valtteri Bottas in the car and outgunned his much more celebrated teammate.

On the credit side, Lewis did notch five runners-up spots that season, a feat in itself given the supremacy of Verstappen in the Red Bull. Hamilton's best performance was arguably in France, in July 2022. As a sidenote to his runner-up finish, he became the sixth driver in history to start 300 Grands Prix as he lined up at the French Grand Prix.

His podium finish, allied with Russell's third place, proved to be Mercedes' best joint result of the campaign thus far. Afterwards, an emotional Hamilton told reporters,

'This is my 300th Grand Prix. Obviously, it was mentioned at the beginning of the weekend, and I didn't really think much of it. But today, I woke up feeling so grateful, thinking about all the people that have been with me along the way. For Ron Dennis and Mercedes giving me the chance when I was young. Martin Whitmarsh. Mansour Ojjeh. Toto Wolff, Niki Lauda.

'All incredible people who've supported me since I was 13. To then have this just incredible journey with them, every race powered by Mercedes.

'Collectively as a team, we didn't have the pace of the lead cars . . . but this is an incredible result for us, for George and I to be here. This is progress.'

Also, to his credit, Hamilton spent much of the season helping the engineers as they tried to fine-tune the W13 car. Early in 2022, Mercedes admitted that he often ran radical set-ups to help the engineers understand the W13's problems. It meant he sometimes sacrificed his own performance in practice or even races, while Russell ran on a more stable set-up.

In Saudi Arabia, for example, Hamilton's experimental set-ups backfired, leaving him further down the starting grid than Russell. He had exited after the first round of qualifying because of his experiments – the first time he'd done so since 2017.

He admitted his 'errors' when speaking to Sky Sports F1: 'I don't know how different the cars are set up, but the car was undriveable with the set-up I chose. But it's my own fault; I made some set-up changes. I don't know if that was everything to do with it, but it was very unstable. I don't know what I'm going to be able to do tomorrow, but I'm a long way back. I just apologised to my team. Everyone works so hard and when you don't deliver for them, it's gutting.'

A further ignominy was that the record books would show 2022 to be just the third time in 16 seasons that Lewis had been beaten by a teammate. George Russell joined a list that included Jenson Button (2011 at McLaren) and Nico Rosberg (2016 at Mercedes).

Disappointing as it was, both Hamilton and Russell outscored Norris that season – by almost double, or more, his total points. Lando, like Lewis, had suffered because the car wasn't up to the job. But the intriguing f1mathematicalmodel.com/site, which rates drivers over the season, considering metrics such as age and relative experience, as well as points gained, found Lando's season wasn't bad at all, everything taken into account. He finished high up on the scale, fourth, with this summary to explain why: 'Lando Norris is not only very highly rated by the model but also one of the most consistent drivers on the grid. Only fellow Brit and prodigy, George Russell, scored closer to his personal maximum in 2022. Norris does, however, beat out Russell on pace and is projected to have the higher ceiling. The most impressive thing about Lando is still his reliability, even in the face of his undeniable speed.

'Since his rookie season he has been becoming uncharacteristically spotless for a young driver. He halved his deficit with every season, so far. If this trend holds true, he will end the 2023 season with a deficit of around 0.8, putting him at 86.7.'

In comparison, George finished sixth and Lewis fifth within the intriguing system – so maybe it wasn't as bad a campaign as it seemed when analysing traditional stats and outcomes for the trio.

No matter. It's fair to say that all three Brits were weary and needed a good relaxing break at the end of the season. And they were all hoping promised improvements to their cars would pay dividends as 2023 dawned.

The question on most F1 pundits' lips as the new season began in Bahrain in the March of that year was simple: could Lewis Hamilton ever reclaim his perch at the top, or were we now in the unstoppable Verstappen era? The inevitable second question followed. If Mercedes couldn't provide him with a car to seriously challenge Max, would he finally, seriously, consider a move to Ferrari, which he had long admitted was his dream move?

There was clearly much at stake as they lined up on the grid on 5 March in the desert heat. Unfortunately, any optimism would drain away during the campaign as it turned out to be the second successive season Hamilton would not record a single win.

However, he did make the podium on six occasions. He finished runner-up in Australia, Spain and the USA – and third in Canada, Britain and Mexico. Lewis also grabbed pole in Hungary. The results meant he would end the season in third in the Drivers' Championship, with 234 points, behind Red Bull's Sergio Perez. The champion was, of course, Mr Verstappen . . . now firmly out on his own as top dog in F1.

Lewis also finished ahead of teammate George Russell, so had the consolation of regaining his position as number one at Mercedes in terms of season's end results. But for such a garlanded individual, it was still a sad fact that at the end of the 2023 season, his most recent F1 win had come at the 2021 Saudi Arabian Grand Prix. He would tell reporters that the highlight in 2023 was when he won pole in Hungary – the only time since 2021 that he had come out tops in qualifying.

Lewis explained, 'I think obviously Budapest was the highlight, a track that I love and somehow to dethrone the Red Bull for a single moment gave us a lot of hope. And that knowing that if we just keep pushing we may get there.'

It sounded like a man whistling in the wind, not a genius of the track. The Mercedes was no slouch, but it paled in comparison to the all-conquering Red Bull. And Ferrari and McLaren were also starting to get their act together.

Lewis saw some consolation in that, despite his own barren season in terms of wins, he had pushed the W14 car to its limits – and would finish third overall in the final drivers' standings. A definite improvement on the sixth place of the previous year.

But towards the end of the season, he couldn't hide his frustration as the car once again showed its inconsistency. Talking to the press pack after the sprint race in Brazil, he admitted, 'It was horrible. It was not enjoyable whatsoever. I was just fighting the car from very early on. The last couple of races we've been excited that we're progressing, and it's been really positive to see. But then you come to another track, and you have the worst drag that you've had for ages. So, it's like you just don't know what to expect with this one.'

He admitted he'd be glad to see the back of the 2023 campaign. 'But only a couple more races with this car and it's gone, and I'll be happy. This year, it's [a case of] just counting down the days, trying to enjoy every day as best we can.'

George finished a disappointing eighth in the Drivers' Championship in 2023, with 175 points, notching just two podiums across the season – in Spain and Abu Dhabi. He summed up his campaign as 'a very, very strange one', adding, 'It's been a season where we've had a lot of pace at times, but never achieved the results that I felt were deserved or were possible. So, we definitely need to try and understand why that was. There's been a huge number of missed opportunities in many regards. It really hasn't been a smooth season. But I think when everything's flowing, when everything's working right, luck tends to be on your side.

'But when, you know, you're on the back foot, you tend to have bad luck. I'm not one for believing in luck. I think you make your own luck. So, we just need to be faster and lady luck will be with us.

'The results were so smooth-flowing last year; I think we finished in the top five more than any other driver. And this year, I feel that I've upped my game in my qualifying pace and upped my game in my race pace, and we've been on the back foot.

'But we have had more competition this year. With

McLaren joining the fight in the second half, Aston being there at the start of the season.'

Mercedes had started 2023 with the W14 carrying over the flawed zero-sidepod design from the year before and hopes of a recovery quickly faded. The car lacked stability, particularly in cornering, and Hamilton and Russell were left chasing Red Bull and even losing ground to Aston Martin and Ferrari at times.

A major upgrade came at Monaco and Spain, where Mercedes abandoned the old concept and introduced sidepods along with suspension and floor changes.

The car became more predictable and podium-capable, but it was never a true match for Red Bull. Hamilton extracted more consistency and points, while Russell often lost out through bad luck or small mistakes. The upgrades steadied the ship but did not deliver a genuine title challenge.

Lando upped his game, in no small part due to the improvement in the McLaren. He was sixth in the Drivers' Championship with 205 points. He had no wins, but seven podium finishes. Best finishes were second places. Norris himself called 2023 'his best year' so far, citing improvements in tyre management and consistency. In an exclusive interview with Motorsport.com, he said, 'I think it's been my best year. I think it's been our best year as a team. I guess a lot of it's just for the obvious reasons – the success that we've been able to have after the start that we've had.

'I think there's been a lot of great performances – both in terms of just racing through and having some good ones. Mexico is probably the highlight of all of that.'

Lando confirmed his position as number one at McLaren, although Oscar Piastri was now asking questions of him as he became more confident in his second season in F1. Like Lando and Lewis, he was a newbie who wasn't at all content at simply having earned a drive in the top tier of motorsport: he wanted to be the main man.

His and Lando's 2023 season had hinged on McLaren's mid-year upgrades. The MCL60 began the campaign slow and uncompetitive, but the improvements by the time of the Austrian GP marked a turning point. With improved aerodynamics and efficiency, the car suddenly found front-running pace. Norris, who had been fighting in the midfield, was now a regular podium contender, and Piastri also benefited with strong finishes. The transformation was one of the most dramatic in recent F1 history, turning McLaren from a struggling outfit into Red Bull's most consistent challenger by the latter half of the year. Norris's strength was being consistently near top positions even when not winning. Russell had some podiums but also 'off' weekends. Hamilton had high expectations, but the Mercedes still wasn't good enough to claim wins or challenge for the title.

And all three Brits had one other major issue to contend with all season in 2023 – Verstappen. The Dutchman dominated with 19 wins, which meant that in many races the competition for second and third was the realistic target for Hamilton, Norris and Russell.

And so on to 2024 for our generational British trio, and the season when McLaren and Norris truly started to make waves in F1.

The team arrived as a top-tier outfit, winning races, securing the constructors' title and proving a consistent threat right across the season. But 2023 had been essential to this success: it wasn't overnight. Without the upgrades, restructuring and performance gains in that year, McLaren wouldn't have been poised for the leap in 2024. In a nutshell, 2023 was the rehearsal; 2024 was the breakthrough.

Their car for 2024, the MCL38, proved much more competitive. Early in the season there were strong signs – podiums, wins, strong qualifying pace. Key upgrades to aerodynamics, tyre wear and suspension paid off. Their performances and results improved significantly, with race wins arriving.

The Constructors' Championship was their first since 1998. McLaren's official site summed it up like this: 'After a nail-biting finish to the 2024 Formula 1 season, we secured our ninth Formula 1 Constructors' Championship at the Abu Dhabi Grand Prix. This year's V6 hybrid McLaren MCL38 proved stunningly quick in the hands of our drivers Lando Norris and Oscar Piastri, racking up six race wins and 21 podiums throughout the 2024 season. The title came down to the final race in Abu Dhabi and saw the team score 26 constructors' points and secure the championship.'

Lando Norris was top dog among our three Brit aces in 2024. OK, he was secondbest behind Verstappen, but the Dutchman was still so ahead of the pack that second really did feel like first. Lando showed his mettle with four wins and 13 podiums. Teammate Piastri also gave warning of his potential for 2025, with two wins and eight podiums.

George Russell had a solid season, securing two wins and four podiums. Lewis Hamilton scored two wins and five podiums. But Russell finished sixth to Hamilton's seventh in the championship by virtue of picking up consistent points finishes when he wasn't on the podium – while Hamilton had more low-scoring or non-scoring races.

Mercedes was still able to achieve decent results, mainly in qualifying and a handful of races. Hamilton stayed strong, yet his dominance and consistency fell short, and Russell took advantage, particularly in qualifying. Lewis still managed wins and podiums, using his years of experience to keep in touch with his two rival British 'whippersnappers'.

The 2024 swansong, and Hamilton's swansong at Mercedes, came at Abu Dhabi. As an indication of what was to come the following season, Lando roared home to victory while Lewis was fourth and George fifth.

It was a final defiant stand by Hamilton: he wasn't going gently into that good night. No way.

He had started 16th on the grid and even had the cojones to overtake George on the last lap to secure fourth, his final result for the team.

The final radio message between Lewis, his race engineer Peter 'Bono' Bonnington and Toto Wolff was emotional and moving . . .

Bonnington: Have to say, mate; it's been epic working with you.

Wolff: Lewis, that was the drive of a world champion. That was the drive of a world champion. Amazing.

Hamilton: Thanks, Toto. That was fun.

Bonnington: Good man, stellar job today, bud. But yeah, it's been a pleasure all the way.

Hamilton: Yeah, Bono. We dreamed alone, but together we believed. And as a team, we achieved things. Thank you for all the courage, the determination, the passion, and for seeing me and supporting me. What started out as a leap of faith turned into a journey into the history books. We did everything together and I'm so, so grateful to everyone. Both here and back at the factory. From the bottom of my heart, all the best.

Bonnington: Thank you, Lewis. Yeah, it's been an amazing journey, and so grateful to be a part of this chapter of your life, and best of luck for the next one.

Hamilton: I love you guys, I really, really do.

Wolff: We love you too and you are always going to be part of this family. And if we can't win, you should win.

There was no getting away from the fact that, in pure stats terms, this had been Hamilton's worst ever F1 season, with that seventh-place finish in the championship. But at least he exited Mercedes with a final-flourish after overhauling Russell for that fourth-place spot in his last race. He admitted it meant a lot to him to have signed off with some pride after a tough final campaign, 'I just didn't give up, kept pushing. But I had a massive gap to close, so I just focused on getting absolutely everything from the car and not giving up. I just wanted to finish on as high as possible and just give every ounce of me to the team as they've given to me all of these years.

'All my races have been powered by Mercedes, and all the

success we've had. I just sat there to think about all that and just contemplate how great a journey it's been. I'm going to miss them – I can't tell you how much I'm going to miss them; it's going to be a huge amount. I've worked with them every day for the past 12 years. There's a lot of love within this team, and that's not going anywhere.'

George was generous in his praise of his teammate, even as he lost out to him in their final race together. He told reporters, 'Lewis had an amazing race, so I want to say a big well done to him. He has not only been an incredible teammate, but someone that I looked up to when I was karting and racing in junior formula. He is not only the greatest driver of all time but is the type of person that every racing driver should aspire to be. I wish him well in his next challenge and look forward to battling him on track.'

He also congratulated Lando on his win and offered his 'congratulations to McLaren on winning the Constructors' Championship . . . they have been a worthy adversary all season and are deserving winners'.

It linked the three Brits together, but it would be Lando who had the final word – and who issued an ominous warning to his two home rivals after he won in Abu Dhabi. On the team radio, he said, 'You all deserve this [the race win and the constructors' title win]. Thank you so much. It's been a special year. Next year is going to be my year too.'

CHAPTER 13

THE PROMISED LAND

So, after a journey that has taken us from the '60s, with the likes of Jim Clark, Jackie Stewart and Graham Hill, through the '70s and James Hunt, the '80s with Nigel Mansell, the '90s with Damon Hill and David Coulthard, we finally arrive at the promised land. The moment our three British heroes of the modern era — Hamilton, Norris and Russell — finally converge in 2025 for the fiercest of battles, both inwards and outwards, for supremacy, prestige and personal pride.

As Hamilton dominated up until 2020, his relative demise in 2025 had coincided with the continued rise of Norris and Russell. Of course, the cars have a lot of say in this: while Norris's McLaren had now proved the one to beat, Russell's Mercedes was still generally there or thereabouts, while valid questions continue to be asked about Hamilton's Ferrari.

And in the mind of many pundits, about the fire in his belly, and whether he was finally feeling his age, at 40.

These are all fair questions although my reading is that the fire will never diminish for Lewis Hamilton. He will always want to win and will be a winner if you give him the tools to complete the job. In 2025, he wasn't too old; he was simply adapting to the idiosyncrasies of a brand-new team (and Ferrari had also been entangled with a whole raft of struggles and battles to become a force again, while constantly beholden to nods to a gloried past. A bit like Manchester United in the world of football).

But until the conclusion of Lewis's last season at Mercedes in 2024, there wasn't a massive difference in the trio's trajectories. I'd argue Lewis, George and Lando were of equal billing that season, after previous years of ups and downs for all three.

For sure, Hamilton suffered a crisis of confidence after that criminal final day title loss to Verstappen in 2021. He should have been celebrating an eighth world title but instead was left lamenting how cruelly the ultimate accolade would be snatched from him. In the darkest of moments, he would even consider leaving the sport that had been his whole life . . . was his whole life.

A look at the results of the seasons after that shock loss show the virtual equanimity on the racetrack that our three Brits experienced, both in highs and lows. In 2022, Hamilton endured his first winless season ever, often running experimental set-ups. Russell outscored Hamilton and claimed his maiden win in Brazil. Norris was the only non-Red Bull/Ferrari/Mercedes driver to score a podium. Lewis finished sixth in the Drivers' Championship, George fourth and Lando seventh. Not much difference there.

In 2023, Hamilton found a second wind, a new belief, and bounced back with a win and more consistency, outperforming Russell. Russell had strong pace but struggled to convert it into results. Norris had his best season yet, with multiple podiums and a clear edge over rookie teammate Oscar Piastri. It wasn't enough for Lewis to clinch his eighth championship, but he did finish a credible third. George disappointed, with an eighth spot finish, while Lando moved up a spot from the previous campaign, ending up sixth. So, a bit of a topsy-turvy season for the trio, ups and downs but arguably still not that far apart when the reliability of cars and backup team efficiency was taken into account.

Their driving skills and talents remained on something of a par, bar the occasional high or hiccup.

In 2024, there was a discernible movement upwards for Norris, while Hamilton regressed and Russell showed steady progress and managed to outshine Lewis. Some pundits claimed it was because Mercedes prioritised Russell over Hamilton, the thinking being, 'George is our future, Lewis will be our past.'

In his final season at Mercedes, Hamilton finished seventh in the championship, with 223 points. He notched two wins (Silverstone and Spa), five podiums, one sprint win (China), but was out-qualified by teammate Russell in 19 of 24 races. So, his swansong with Mercedes could probably be described as solid but not spectacular.

He showed flashes of brilliance – especially with that brilliant home win at Silverstone – but wouldn't have been happy to be generally outpaced by his younger teammate. His final year marked the end of an era for both him and Mercedes before his move to Ferrari in 2025.

Russell finished sixth with 245 points. He also enjoyed two wins (Austria and Las Vegas), had four podiums and four pole positions. He didn't win any sprints but stepped up as Mercedes' number one, narrowly edging out Hamilton in points and qualifying.

His win in Las Vegas was particularly dominant and he was more consistent across the season. Despite internal team drama and uncertainty with Hamilton's departure, George proved he was ready to lead the Silver Arrows into the post-Lewis era. It looked as if he was all set to challenge Lando Norris for the title.

As for Lando, in 2024, he chalked up his best F1 campaign, up to that moment in time. He finished runner-up in the Drivers' Championship to Verstappen, with 374 points. That glory run included four wins (including Miami and Abu Dhabi), 13 podiums, eight pole positions and one sprint win. His successes played a major part as McLaren also stormed to victory in the Constructors' Championship – their first since 1998.

It was a career-defining season for Lando. With McLaren's upgraded MCL38, he consistently challenged for wins. His performances were mature, aggressive and technically spot-on – repaying McLaren for their faith in him over the years and suggesting there could be even greater glory times to come.

After the final race, Lando's words to the McLaren team highlighted his belief that this could be just the beginning of a new era of dominance for them, after years in the wilderness. He said, 'A big thank you goes to everyone at McLaren, everyone in papaya, everyone who supported us this year. It's been tough, but for us to win the Constructors' Championship after 26 years is pretty special.'

There was also a sense of jubilation in the end-of-season statement put out by McLaren: 'Taking the 2024 Formula 1 constructors' title has shown once again that we have a World Championship mindset – and it's been that way from the start. Founded in 1963 as a small, committed racing team, we won the very first championship we entered, when our founder Bruce McLaren triumphed in the 1964 Tasman Series held in New Zealand and Australia. By 1968, we were winning races in Formula 1, and since then we've won 12 Formula 1 Drivers' Championships and now nine Constructors' Championships.'

The inference was that the newly won constructors' title was just the start: now for the drivers' title.

On paper at least, it seemed the only true threat to Lando's hopes of achieving that would come close to home. As the 2025 campaign progressed, it looked like his main rival wouldn't be Hamilton, Russell or even Verstappen.

However, by the October of 2025, fans and pundits were wondering aloud whether Max might yet pull off an almost miraculous fifth title success. Consecutive wins and the idea that McLaren could be feeling more pressure added to the debate.

Plus, a floor upgrade introduced at Monza appeared to have boosted the performance of Verstappen's Red Bull car.

Yet it remained more likely that teammate Piastri would prove the biggest obstacle to Lando storming to his first F1 drivers' crown – as the McLaren duo's lead over Max remained a formidable obstacle to the Dutchman's hopes.

After Monza, in September, Piastri led the way with 324 points, Lando was second with 293 points – 31 points behind Piastri – while Max was third on 230 points, 94 points behind Piastri. With only eight races (and three sprints) remaining, it meant Norris had much to do if he was to overwhelm Piastri. He would need to outperform the Australian significantly over the remainder of the season. Verstappen's battle was even tougher – he needed a near-perfect run, including multiple wins and sprint victories plus several poor results or retirements from Piastri to close the gap. It was mathematically possible, but unlikely.

Champion or runner-up, Lando would have proved yet again that he was in the reckoning. And his duel with Piastri draws together another strand with one of our main protagonists in this book: Hamilton, and his rivalry with Alonso, in 2007. As we noted earlier on, Alonso joined McLaren as a two-time world champion in 2007 but his time with the team was short-lived and marked by a strained relationship with the team and Hamilton. He lasted just one season before returning to Renault.

Not that either Lando or Oscar were expected to flounce out in 2025. Both guys were ambitious and determined, but respectful, whereas neither Lewis nor Fernando cared much about the other's welfare or feelings when it came to racing. Their rivalry was intense, and no holds barred.

Yet in one sense there was perhaps a similarity. Just as Lewis had been nurtured over the years by McLaren, so too had Lando. And just as Alonso was viewed as an outsider in that he arrived late, perhaps so was Oscar. While Lando entered F1 in 2019, aged 19, so Oscar did in 2022, aged 21, starting as Alpine's reserve driver. A year later, he joined McLaren after rejecting an Alpine promotion. The move was controversial.

On 1 August 2022, Fernando Alonso (there he is again!) shocked Alpine by announcing he was leaving to join Aston Martin for 2023. Alpine suddenly had a vacant race seat and moved quickly. The following day, they issued a press release, saying, 'Oscar Piastri will drive for the Alpine F1 Team in 2023, replacing Fernando Alonso.'

But they hadn't secured Oscar's signature, and he had already been negotiating with McLaren behind the scenes. Hours later, Piastri himself posted on social media: 'I understand that, without my agreement, Alpine have put out a press release late this afternoon that I am driving for them next year. This is wrong, and I have not signed a contract with Alpine for 2023. I will not be driving for Alpine next year.'

It was unprecedented: a driver publicly rejecting a team's official announcement. Both Alpine and McLaren claimed to have a valid contract with Piastri and the dispute went to the FIA's Contract Recognition Board. On 2 September 2022, the CRB unanimously decided in McLaren's favour.

He was their man. The incident showed Piastri's inner strength, refusing to be pushed about, or to drive for a second-choice team.

As he battled Lando for the title in 2025, he would once again show this inner steel. His GP wins highlighted his calmness and composure under severe pressure, and he immediately matched Norris for pace. Suddenly, Lando's long-awaited title breakthrough was not under direct threat from Hamilton or Russell or Verstappen . . . but from inside his own garage.

On the surface, it appeared the young Aussie had come from nowhere to rival Lando, but his two previous seasons at McLaren had signposted his threat. In his rookie campaign, in 2023, he finished ninth in the standings, scored two podiums and won the Qatar Sprint Race, his first F1 victory of any kind.

A year later, he established himself as a consistent front-runner, often matching or outpacing Lando.

And after Monza, in 2025, he was leading the championship after seven Grand Prix wins, and was odds-on to become Australia's first F1 world champion since Alan Jones in 1980.

Piastri's background had traces of Norris's in not having money worries as he attempted to make a name for himself, Russell's for one motoring feat, and Hamilton's for his immediate impact in F1, and rivalry with an established teammate once there.

Born on 6 April 2001, he grew up in Melbourne, Australia. His father, Chris Piastri, founded HP Tuners, a successful automotive software company. The business funded Oscar's early racing career, reportedly contributing up to A$6.5 million. This parallels Lando, whose father was a wealthy businessman and supported his motorsport journey.

Dad Chris was also Oscar's mechanic during his early days in the sport.

The upbringing in an upmarket area was also similar to Lando – in this case the pleasant, affluent Melbourne suburb, Brighton. Kervale, a property developer in Brighton, spoke of the area in dazzling terms: 'Sparkling Brighton Beach with its colourful bathing boxes are among Melbourne's most iconic images. But with easy access to the Melbourne Central Business District, designer shopping, buzzing cafes and plenty of outdoor activities, there are plenty of reasons why Brighton is the city's premium beachside lifestyle.'

'For buyers on the hunt for the best of bayside living, it's hard to go past Brighton,' explained Cameron Kusher, economist, REA Group. 'Brighton is a really popular lifestyle suburb, right on Port Phillip Bay. It attracts premium property developments, high property prices and rental prices – but there are lots of very good reasons for that.'

According to Oscar's mum, Nicole, her son profited from a very rich cultural background, too. Speaking to the *Red Flags* podcast in 2024, she revealed, 'So people jump on the Italian because of the "Piastri", which is Italian, but he's just as much Chinese as he's Italian. It's a long way back; it's not like no one was born in Italy. So, Chris's grandfather was Italian, and Chris's grandmother, whom he was married to, was Chinese.

'Yeah, people pick up on the Piastri, of course, but he's just as much Chinese. So, it's like a long way back. My side is Scottish and Irish. Yeah, that's my side, which he probably doesn't even know about.'

Well, he certainly did after the podcast. And if he did win the title in 2025, Scots and Irish F1 fans could celebrate his success with a genuine connection.

Piastri had no funding problems and none on the karting track, either.

From 2011 to 2015, he raced in Australia, then moved to Europe in 2015 to test himself against better karters.

In 2016, his first in Formula 4 UAE, he finished as runner-up. The following year he was runner-up again, this time in the British F4 championship. By 2019 – when Lando was about to embark on his debut F1 season – Piastri had become the Formula Renault Eurocup champion. He was acknowledged for a triple junior titles success as he then added the 2020 Formula 3 and 2021 Formula 2 crowns to his collection.

Part of that accumulation links him with George Russell – both men, along with Charles Leclerc, are the only drivers ever to win F3 and F2 back to back as a rookie. When George won the former in 2017, it was known as GP3. But it became F3 the following season, in much the same way as say football's European Cup became known as the European Champions League.

Then came Oscar's entry into F1, and the link with Hamilton, in that here he was in 2025, still a relative novice in F1, yet competing against established McLaren star Norris for the world title. Just as Lewis had done with Alonso in 2007, also at McLaren.

There are differences: Hamilton joined a McLaren team already fighting at the front in 2007. Piastri got his seat at McLaren when they were rebuilding, in 2023, and only in 2024–25 did the car become championship-capable.

Hamilton was big news when he started out as there had been much hype about him being Ron Dennis's 'project' at McLaren and, with him being the first black driver in F1, the spotlight was intense immediately. By contrast, Piastri's arrival and progress was quieter; he almost hid behind the headlines that Lando was creating as the 'great British hope'.

Hamilton became world champion in his second full season, in 2008. As this book was published, Piastri was leading the standings in just his third full season.

But the rivalry with Norris differs to the one Lewis had with Alonso.

As outlined in an earlier chapter, Alonso was signed from Renault as the reigning double world champion, and McLaren intended him to be the de facto number one driver . . . and so did the Spaniard. Hamilton, though a rookie, was expected to learn quietly. The problem was, he immediately matched Alonso for pace. Alonso didn't like this as he had expected to be treated as a double world champion; not being left red-faced by an insolent young rookie. He turned to Ron Dennis to put Hamilton in his rightful place, but Ron didn't, or more likely couldn't, given Lewis's inbuilt determination, and speed.

The situation spiralled out of control, crushing the traditional 'number one/number two' structure. Alonso felt undermined, Hamilton refused to play a support role, and the team split into factions. The bad blood and disputes arguably contributed to McLaren missing out on the Drivers' Championship title that year, with Kimi Räikkönen scooping it for Ferrari.

It was a much different, calmer sea as McLaren set sail in 2025.

Both team and drivers were determined there would be no repeat. Lando and Oscar began the season talking openly about wanting to beat the other – but that it was all-important to put the team first. Clearly, they had been briefed about that. McLaren bosses, Andrea Stella and Zak Brown, had made it clear they wouldn't allow any rivalry to break team spirit.

That may have followed on from a spat in Hungary the previous campaign. Then, McLaren had pitted Norris on Lap 17, one lap before Piastri. This gave Norris the undercut, a strategic advantage where fresher tyres allowed him to gain time while Piastri remained on worn ones. As a result, Norris rejoined the track ahead of his teammate, despite Piastri having led the race. McLaren later asked Norris to reverse the order, restoring fairness. Initially resistant, Norris questioned the decision over team radio but eventually complied on Lap 68.

The switch allowed Piastri to win his first Grand Prix and highlighted McLaren's commitment to team-first racing principles.

Piastri felt it had been the correct decision. 'The longer

you leave it, of course, the more you get a bit nervous. But it was well executed by the team. And yeah, I think it was the right thing. I put myself in the right position at the start. And yeah, with the different strategy we had, yes, my pace probably wasn't as quick as I would have liked in the last stint, but I was still in the right position to make it happen. So yeah, well executed from the team.'

Norris kept his opinion short and simple, 'The team asked me to do it, so I did it. And that's it.'

In 2025, a couple of incidents at the end of August and first week of September encapsulated the team and drivers' determination to put team health and integrity above all else.

At the Dutch GP, on the last day of the month, Lando suffered a real blow to his championship hopes when he had to retire due to a mechanical fault. With just seven laps remaining, he had been running second behind Oscar when his hopes literally seemed to go up in smoke. An oil leak led to smoke and fire spewing from the car. His race engineer Will Joseph tried to console him: 'Sorry, mate, you were fast today, you were really fast.' Lando replied, 'Doesn't matter.' But Will insisted, 'I know, but you were fast.' Lando said, 'I know, I know. Unlucky, boys. Unlucky.'

With Oscar winning the race, it left Lando 34 points adrift in the championship. Team principal Andrea Stella told the press that the problem would be fixed before Monza the following week, but also recognised that the malfunction could prove costly for Norris. He said, 'This is the first technical problem for the team after a long run of faultless reliability. Reliability has been a strong point at McLaren for a long time; we have had today what looks like a technical reliability problem, which is always disappointing.

'But I would say that it is even more inconvenient because it affects a situation in which we, as a team, wanted to stay as neutral as possible in what is the drivers' individual quests in the Drivers' Championship. So, it is not ideal.'

He tried to cool the heat by suggesting that rather than a setback, Lando could perhaps view it as a challenge to illustrate what a world-class driver he now was. 'If anything, we may see even a better version of Lando because now is the time to extract if there is anything more, even more out of his potential. So, I look forward to seeing Lando in the coming races. I'm sure this is going to be a great spectacle for Formula 1 and if anything, it's going to make the competition with Oscar even more interesting. We know that his [Lando's] talent is immense and I'm sure this situation in the championship will give him extra motivation to try and extract it.'

And there was no gloating from Oscar, just realism in an acceptance that nothing had been settled yet: far from it, in fact. 'There's still a long way to go. I need to keep pushing and trying to win races. I wouldn't say it's a very comfortable margin. As we saw today, it can change with one DNF very quickly. So this far out from the end of the year, it's not a comfortable gap.'

It was all so very different to the squabbles, recriminations and accusations thrown around the McLaren garage in 2007, as Lewis and Fernando battled to be top dog. When Lando was interviewed by reporters after the DNF, he was naturally disappointed, but philosophical. He said, 'It was unlucky, but I just want to move on, to go have a burger and go home. It wasn't my fault, so there's nothing I can really do. It's just not my weekend. A little bit unlucky yesterday with the wind [in qualifying] and unlucky today. Tough one. Of course, it's frustrating. It hurts a bit from a championship point of view. It's a lot of points to lose so quickly and so easily. That's life, so that's why I just take it on the chin and move on.' Yet despite his own disappointment, he only had praise for his teammate, adding, 'The only thing I can do is try to win every race. That's going to be difficult, but I'll make sure I give it everything I can.

'I have a good teammate – he's strong, he's quick in every situation, every scenario. It's hard to get things back on someone who is just good in pretty much every situation.

'It certainly hasn't helped [the DNF]. It's a lot of points to lose so quickly and so easily. Nothing I can control now, but it's almost a big enough gap that I can just chill out about it and go for it.'

It meant Piastri had seven wins to Norris's five for the season as they headed to Monza for the next instalment, but the most important stats were those 34 points differences in the championship. They arrived in Italy and still there was no visible stress or strains. Indeed, Lando went out of his way to emphasise to the press that he only wanted to win the title by fair means, not foul. He said, 'I can still win the championship without anything happening to Oscar. That's the way I want to do it. It would make my life easier if there were more drivers in between [us] every now and then. The thing is, we're so dominant as a team and that almost makes my life harder.

'It's pretty easy to go, "Well, that's life, you know what I can do. If I lose the championship by those points, I'll just have to keep my chin up, my head up high and try to do it again next year." I can't dwell on those moments too much. It's not anyone's fault. Even if it was, I just have to take it on the chin and move on. I've got to be on it a bit more and sharp with various things here and there. But I can't do a lot more as I feel I'm already doing everything I can.'

Lando would cut the points deficit to 31 at Monza, as a direct result of that team ethic.

He had been leading Oscar when he went to pit on lap 46. Oscar had pitted for soft tyres the previous lap. However, Lando's stop was delayed by a front-left wheel issue, causing him to fall behind Piastri when he rejoined the race. McLaren then told Oscar to give the position back to Lando – in line with their 'values and principles' approach. Max Verstappen won the race, but the radio request and swapping of positions meant that Norris was second and Piastri third.

Afterwards, McLaren team principal Andrea Stella said there would be a review so they could continue their 'foundation of pursuing excellence'. He added, 'If you think that whatever you do is good and you are not going to have an individual or a team review of anything you do, even the things you do perfectly, you're simply not going to progress. For me, reviewing . . . [means] potentially we will further align on them [principles] and we will confirm them. So, the fact that I use this word doesn't mean that there will be changes . . . it does apply in the way you go racing with your drivers.'

It suggested that far from there being any watering down of principles, they would become even more firmly entrenched as the company's central ethical ideology.

He also explained the reasoning behind the race switch: 'The pit stop situation is not only a matter of fairness, but also a matter of consistency with our principles. However the championship goes, what's important is the championship runs within the principles and the racing fairness we have at McLaren.

'The fact that we went first with Oscar, compounded by the slow pit stop with Lando, led to a swap of positions and we thought it was absolutely the right thing to go back to the situation pre-existing the pit stop and then let the guys race.'

It was certainly an intriguing scenario as we prepared for the run-in Grands Prix that would result in Lando becoming Britain's new world champion, or his Aussie teammate swiping the glory that the boy from Bristol so desperately sought. Or perhaps even Verstappen pulling off a miraculous turnaround, and winning it. If he didn't succeed, Lando had already vowed he'd be more determined the following season.

As Lando battled for the world crown, George Russell sparked mixed opinions about his progression to the very top. By the time Monza was packed away in September 2025, critics and fans often had polarised views on the man who was now number one at Mercedes. One F1 fan summed up the backing for George, saying, 'He has arguably been the driver of the season thus far and if Merc gets some upgrade packages right, he could compete for a drivers' title. Big if because the McLarens are a step ahead but it's possible.'

While another spoke for the other side, who still had doubts: 'Russell has done pretty well with the car, but I don't think he's a championship calibre driver. He'd need an exquisite car for that and a bit of quality lacking on the competition's cars.'

Some fans even questioned if maybe George wasn't as happy as imagined at Mercedes. Maybe the car not matching the McLaren for speed, or even the Red Bull, was a problem, or maybe he didn't feel as valued as he should, given he hadn't been awarded a new contract by September 2025. Or that he had been unhappy at suggestions that the team had had talks with Max Verstappen and that he might join as their new number one – claims Mercedes boss Toto Wolff had been at pains to deny.

But in April 2025, George had laughed off suggestions he was worried about his future, given his contract would have run out at the end of the season. He said, 'From my side, there's literally no stress, no worries whatsoever. When it comes to contracts, everyone gets so excited about it, but the fact is, drivers have had contracts, and if they don't perform, they'll get booted out. For drivers, performance is our currency. That's what we've got. And if you perform, everything's good. So, I'm just excited to go racing this weekend, focus on performance, and the future sorts itself out.'

He said he believed that he would get together with Toto when the time was right, and they would take it from there. There was no sense at all that Toto was unhappy with him. In fact, after George took P3 at August's Hungarian GP, the Mercedes chief made it clear how he appreciated the work his number one was doing.

He told Motorsport.com, 'When I look at George, the development he has made since he joined Formula 1 – from the fast kiddo at Williams, to being drafted into Mercedes, clearly with the greatest of all greats, Lewis Hamilton. You could already see last year he was becoming so strong on pure pace – and in terms of results, the stronger driver. Now, with Lewis having gone to Ferrari, he has taken the senior driver slot, and it happened completely naturally . . . and he delivers.'

It didn't stop fans speculating that potentially there was a rift. 'Neither George nor Mercedes want a very long deal here. Two years is probably what George is aiming for and with Max out of the question, he can push for it. The other question is salary. The rumoured offer of £30 million would make him the third best paid driver on the grid, but he might want more. According to some unreliable rumours, he wanted £50 million so the £30 million salary is still quite off.

'George is probably quite comfortable now that Max is out of the picture. He's quite a smart chap so he knows how much he can push for with Mercedes. The simple answer is, as he's stated numerous times, that they need him and he needs them so they'll probably meet somewhere in the middle.'

Sky's F1 analyst, and ex F1 driver, Martin Brundle felt that George might be feeling 'bruised' after not seeing a new deal on the table by September. He told Nico Rosberg on Sky Sports F1, 'I'd have signed George a long time ago, because George is not happy, is he? It's very easy to see that George feels quite bruised about all the Verstappen talk through the summer. But when you look at the calm at McLaren and other teams, I just think they've injected too many of their own problems into the driver line-up. I'd keep him.

'He's driving so beautifully, George. He just looks the real deal, he's confident. But he said, "I went to Mercedes expecting to win World Championships straight away, relatively straightforwardly." And of course, that's just not happening.'

Former champion Rosberg had no doubts about George's standing. He said, 'I'll agree with you, Martin, that for me, George is top three, at the very least, in terms of driver this year. Phenomenally consistent, so rapid; he is always extracting the maximum from that car. That's why it's so hard for Antonelli [Mercedes number two] also, because he's up against one of the very, very best out there, which doesn't help.'

By September, George said there had been movement on a potential new deal, and that he would love to stay with Toto and Mercedes. He told Sky Sports F1, 'I definitely wanted to take the summer to really think about my future, because it's obviously important for everybody when you're discussing the coming years. The team and Toto were very open to discussing or finding a solution during the break, but I just wanted to take that time.

'There are pros and cons in terms of duration. The truth is, I just want to win, and I want to win with Mercedes. If I could choose, that is what I would choose to do.'

Yet at the start of the season, he had been in little doubt that he faced an uphill fight if he were to become champion. Always a realist, he knew full well that the revitalised, powerful McLaren of the previous season would take some stopping in the current campaign. In an interview with the BBC, he predicted as much, saying, 'I don't think we have the car right now that is potentially capable of beating the McLaren. Without doubt, they look by far the strongest. Their race pace looks pretty impressive.

'There's definitely improvements throughout our car, no doubt about it. Naturally, there's always something you need to work on. We struggled a bit with low-speed understeer last year. There's still signs of that that we're still trying to get on top of, and we think we've got some things in the locker to try and cure those issues. But definitely the car's feeling a bit more together.'

He would be proved correct and the stats by September highlighted why people couldn't agree on just where George stood, or where he was heading. They were far from brilliant but still suggested a push by the team/a team could take him to the next level. Out of 16 races, he had won one, but notched six podiums, with one pole position.

But few could deny he had done a good job given the circumstances in his first season as number one. It was always going to be a difficult task to even attempt to live up to Hamilton's legacy. The seven-time world champion cast a long shadow, and George probably needed a season to throw aside the cobwebs and emerge afresh. On the plus side, in 2025 he consistently dragged Mercedes into podium contention, and his win in Canada showed he could convert pole into victory under pressure. Six podiums in 16 races were surely elite-level, given the car's patchy race pace.

George also had to take on the role of team leader for the first time in his career. Within Mercedes, Toto had dubbed him the top 'number one driver we could wish for'. And within that role, he also had to mentor Kimi Antonelli, an 18-year-old rookie at the start of the season, while delivering results. The young Italian had potential but was very raw. After Monza, even Toto had a go at the lad, saying he was disappointed he finished ninth in his home GP, and adding, 'Underwhelming this weekend. Underwhelming. You can't put the car in the gravel bed and expect to be there. All of the race was underwhelming. It doesn't change anything about my support and confidence in his future because I believe he's going to be very, very, very good. But today was underwhelming.'

Clearly, George had a lot on his plate – his own driving, his contract, mentoring the youngster, a car not quite in the groove, and sporadic clangers by the team. The Mercedes W16 had proved unpredictable: fast in qualifying, but not always able to sustain that speed across a full race. Tyre management was also an issue, leaving Russell unable to defend positions late in races. And team strategy calls occasionally worked against him, with safety cars or mistimed pit stops costing better finishing places.

By September, his results showed both the potential of a driver entering his prime and the frustrations of machinery not yet consistently capable of fighting at the very front. His highlight came in Canada, where he delivered Mercedes their first victory of the season. It was a complete performance: pole on Saturday, strong pace on Sunday and the composure to seize on rivals' mistakes.

For a driver long praised for his professionalism and patience, the win represented that he could do the job. It proved a real boost for the team's morale. Outside of Montreal, he did his best with a car that simply wasn't up to the level of the McLaren and Red Bull. He ensured Mercedes remained in the top table conversation as contenders. And he has rarely spoken out of turn, or been outwardly frustrated, proving himself to be a driver Toto and the team can totally rely on for honesty and integrity. One way of seeing it is that he has been a rock as Mercedes temporarily entered a period of transition. With Hamilton gone and a rookie by his side, plus a car still needing upgrades, George didn't do a bad job. He has become the figure Mercedes can depend on, a driver who represents stability and potential to be the best.

Can he reach the level of Hamilton or Norris? Or will his career be defined by near-misses, strong performances in difficult circumstances, but not the sustained success that his talent suggests is possible? Statistically, he had been outperforming Hamilton, now in the Ferrari, in the 2025 season. By September, he had more podiums, a win, and had been consistently closer to the front.

George didn't appreciate comparisons with Lando; it wasn't fair given that Norris was in the super-fast McLaren. The two drivers are the same generation, both seen as the future of British F1 when they entered the sport. Russell's climb was slower and more methodical, with Williams before moving to Mercedes. Norris was luckier, like Hamilton benefiting from a McLaren education, and developing alongside the team's own revival.

And in 2025, Norris was in a championship fight in a McLaren – with another McLaren driver, which showed the power of the car, whatever the genius of the man in the cockpit. He had multiple wins, regular poles, and a season that looked like the fulfilment of his long-touted potential. Even if he had to wait another season, there was no doubt at all that Lando Norris had arrived, while George Russell was still on his way.

George's Canada victory and overall podium tally were impressive, but he was not in the title race. For pundits and fans, the contrast was stark: one British driver was fighting Piastri and Verstappen for the crown, the other was some way back. That gap was not entirely of his making – Mercedes were rebuilding, while McLaren had given Norris the platform to challenge for the title. But as this book was published, Russell was perhaps more of a dependable contender than a definite champion in the making.

He was doing most things right, but it appeared history

and timing were maybe against him. Hamilton's shadow loomed over his past; Norris's rise defined his present.

His future seemed to depend almost entirely on whether Mercedes would provide him with a car to turn his steady progress into a genuine title challenge. Or maybe, if ultimately, they didn't or couldn't, he would have to go elsewhere to realise his dream of becoming Formula 1 champion.

Lewis Hamilton, meanwhile, had entered 2025 with great hopes of realising his own dream of becoming a F1 champion for an eighth time. He had placed all his eggs, and hopes, of achieving this in one basket: Ferrari, the team he had always dreamed of representing. He had won six world titles at Mercedes, following his debut world crown achieved at McLaren. Now, he had even cut short the new deal he had signed with Mercedes in the summer (via a release clause), which had committed him to staying until at least the end of the 2025 season, to move to 'il Cavallino Rampante'.

Lewis would drive alongside Charles Leclerc on a multi-year deal while Ferrari number two Carlos Sainz would have to find a new role elsewhere. Ferrari had managed to keep a lid on their delight at signing the world's greatest driver, and only initially released a short statement from Maranello when the deal was done: 'Scuderia Ferrari is pleased to announce that Lewis Hamilton will be joining the team in 2025, on a multi-year contract.'

They hadn't won a drivers' world title since Kimi Räikkönen's in 2007 and that had played a big part in their attempts to lure Hamilton. They remain F1's most successful team and the only team to have competed in every World Championship season, so it was hardly a shock that they would want Hamilton. The hope was that, in the swansong of his wonderful career, he could finally bring home the title to them again.

Well, his first season in Italy had not gone at all as the dream script had outlined. It was more of a tentative trot than a prancing horse. By Monza in September, his record at the Italian team made miserable reading: No wins in the 15 Grands Prix so far, no podiums, no pole positions . . . and one Sprint Race triumph, in China. Small pickings indeed for the seven-time world champion. And not much to suggest he might yet scoop that eighth title in 2026, when he would be 41.

Before the race at Monza, with Lewis hoping to find some form in front of the Ferrari home fans, he sat down and told the press just how difficult it had been. He was 42 points behind teammate Charles Leclerc in the title race and had been out-qualified by him ten times, beating him in just two of 15 races – so he didn't sugarcoat his predicament.

Lewis admitted, 'It's been an emotional roller coaster. What can I really say? Did I expect it to be as volatile in terms of the feeling? No, but that's life. And I'd like to think that even though we had a difficult Sunday in Holland last week, we are coming towards the brighter end of the tunnel. I read something recently where it said, "There's no point stressing about tomorrow because it often puts shade on the present."

'So, I'm really trying not to worry about tomorrow.

I'm trying to be present and enjoy every moment because this half of the season has gone by really quickly. There's obviously a long way to go, but I don't want to miss any of these special moments that we're having. Like my first Monza in Ferrari in red and when I leave the garage tomorrow, it's going to be incredibly special coming on to this circuit.

'I want to give the Tifosi [the passionate Ferrari fans] absolutely everything this weekend to get the best result for them because the passion and the support they've given me and this team is like nothing I've ever seen.'

To be fair, he showed signs of a revival in the race that followed. Starting tenth after a five-place penalty, he wound his way through the pack and finished a credible sixth. He was also sixth in the Drivers' Championship on 117 points but trailing fifth-placed Leclerc by 46 points now – a measure of the season's travails.

But there were still backers for the GOAT, including Ferrari team boss Fred Vasseur, who told the media Lewis's battles with George Russell at Monza had seemed to energise him. Once again, our storyline for Hamilton, Russell and Norris was converging.

Vasseur said, 'It was a very good race and I'm very pleased for him because he had a tough time in July and he's back. He's back on the pace. He had a good weekend, a good mood, good approach and I think it will help.

'During the race, he was fighting with Russell until lap 30. That means that he was back in a better position. And I think the energy that he received from the Tifosi on

Wednesday and Thursday in Milano was something very special for him.

'I think this gave him an extra boost all over the weekend. He had to serve the penalty and we knew from the beginning of the weekend that with plus five it's not an easy one, but he came back behind Russell and the pace was there from the first lap of FP1 to the last lap of the race.'

He even said he was confident Lewis would land on the podium before the season's end, but Hamilton 'didn't think so', saying the car still wasn't fast enough, 'Today, Charles was giving it everything. Max is up there now. We don't have the pace of Red Bull or McLaren. So I think we are currently fourth, fifth. If we do an exceptional job, we can maybe get a podium here or there. There's a chance we can have that but in terms of pure pace we don't have that.'

His former boss at Mercedes, Toto Wolff, believed the punters and pundits who were writing him off would be proved wrong. Toto said, 'He has been doubting himself, and we had it in the past [at Mercedes]. When he felt that he had underperformed his own expectations, and the team had its own goal, he's been that emotional, emotionally transparent since he was a young boy, a young adult.

'So, he's going to beat himself up. He's the GOAT. And he will always be the GOAT, and nobody's going to take that away. For sure, no single weekend or race season that hasn't gone to plan [would].'

Prior to joining Ferrari, Lewis had explained on social media just why he had made the move, and what it meant to him. He said it had been a lifelong ambition and that when the chance came, he couldn't turn it down. At his age, it really was a case of now or never. He explained why the team were so special to him: 'Of course, I think for every driver growing up, watching the history, watching Michael Schumacher in his prime, I think probably all of us sit in our garage and see the screen pop up, and you see the driver in the red cockpit and you wonder what it would be like to be surrounded by the red.

'You go to the Italian Grand Prix and you see the sea of red Ferrari fans and you can only stand in awe of that. It's a team that's not had huge success since 2007, and I saw it as a huge challenge. Without a doubt, even as a kid, I used to play on games as Michael in that car, so it definitely is a dream and I'm really, really excited about it.'

That desire to have joined Ferrari, along with his still strong ambition to win that elusive eighth title, along with the motivation to prove the doubters who have written him off as being wrong, suggests to me that there may just be one final act in the remarkable Hamilton story.

As Norris and Russell fight with Piastri to become the new kings of the grid, perhaps there is a twist in the tale least expected.

That in 2026 Hamilton passes on to Lando and George his most treasured gift: to never give in, however bleak the prospects may look of glory. By winning the eighth, he'd leave them with something to hold on to if times get tough, or success doesn't seem to be coming.

A pipe dream, maybe, but Lewis Hamilton's story has

from the very start been the story of the underdog, battling against those more privileged, and coming away victorious. No wonder George and Lando admit they've learned so much from him – just as he had learned from the lineage of previous great Brits like Jim Clark, Stirling Moss and Nigel Mansell. One day, George and Lando may well tell new generations how lucky they were to have driven in the era of the greatest driver of them all – and that his example off the track, and achievements on it, had propelled them to greatness too, after he'd finally gone.